This book belongs to:

Table of Contents

Table of Contents

Unit 1

Words with *l* Blends

1 Say the name of the object out loud.
Fill in the missing ***l*** blend for the word.

a) fl cl

______over

b) gl pl

______anet

c) cl fl

______oud

d) bl pl

______ocks

e) cl fl

______ag

f) pl gl

______asses

g) pl fl

______ane

h) fl gl

______ue

i) bl cl

______ender

j) bl fl
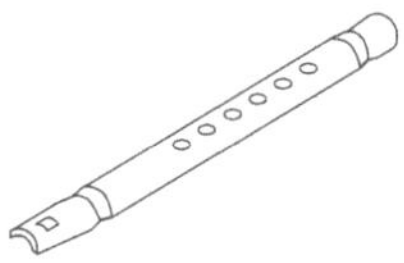
______ute

k) cl bl
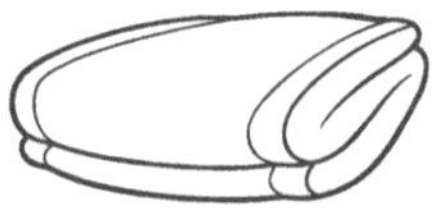
______anket

l) pl gl
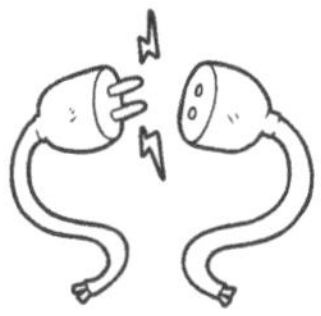
______ug

Words with l Blends (cont.)

2. Fill in the blank using the best word from the list.

clock	clown	club	fly	glass
gloves	plant	plate	sleep	slide

a) I checked the ________________ for the time.

b) I water my ________________ to help it grow.

c) My favourite thing at the park is the ________________.

d) I pour orange juice into a ________________.

e) It's late at night, and it's time to ________________.

f) Peter joined the robotics ________________ at school.

g) Mom puts a ________________ on the table for dinner.

h) There was a funny ________________ at the birthday party.

i) The birds quickly ________________ away.

j) In winter, I put ________________ on my hands.

Unit 2

Words with *r* Blends

1 Say the name of the object out loud.
Fill in the missing *r* blend for the word.

a) pr fr

_____ame

b) dr br

_____ink

c) dr cr

_____own

d) tr br

_____ain

e) cr fr

_____og

f) br tr

_____idge

g) pr cr

_____etzel

h) pr br

_____ead

i) cr dr

_____ayon

j) cr gr

_____apes

k) tr dr

_____um

l) br tr

_____uck

Words with *r* Blends (cont.)

2. Fill in the blank using the best word from the list.

broom	crack	crust	drain	drink
fridge	green	price	trick	trunk

a) Cathy jumps over the ________________ in the sidewalk.

b) I use a ________________ to sweep the floor.

c) Our parrot has ________________ feathers.

d) What is the ________________ of that book?

e) The soap bubbles go down the ________________.

f) Jim got a cold juice box out of the ________________.

g) We put the groceries in the ________________ of the car.

h) After my run, I had a big ________________ of water.

i) My dog does a cool ________________ to get treats.

j) My favourite part of a pie is the ________________.

Words with *s* Blends

1. Say the name of the object out loud.
Fill in the missing ***s*** blend for the word.

a) sm sl

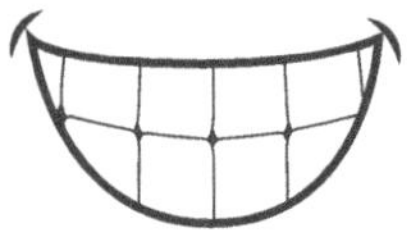

______ile

b) sk sp

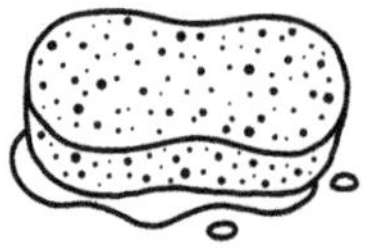

______onge

c) sn sw

______ail

d) st sp

______oon

e) sl sm

______ide

f) st sc

______arf

g) sp sn

______ake

h) sl st

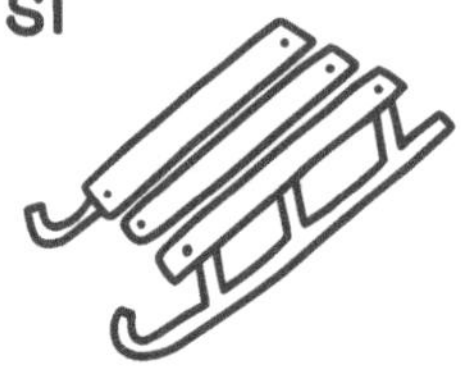

______ed

i) sm sw

______an

j) sk sl

______ates

k) sn sm

______oothie

l) st sk

______ool

Words with s Blends (cont.)

2 Fill in the blank using the best word from the list.

scores	skip	skunk	sloth	smoke
snack	spin	stars	sticker	swim

a) Maple keys ________________ as they fall to the ground.

b) I love to look up at the ________________ at night.

c) Tammy and I ________________ rope at school.

d) When my dad ________________ a goal, we all cheer.

e) A ________________ can let out a very stinky smell.

f) There was ________________ coming from the campfire.

g) A ________________ is an animal that moves slowly.

h) I ate grapes for a ________________ after school.

i) Matt has a very big ________________ collection.

j) Our dog Sally likes to ________________ in the lake.

Unit 4

Words with *sh*

1 Say each word out loud. Look at where a ***sh*** sound can be in a word. Write the correct word beside the picture.

bush	cash	fish	leash	shark
shed	ship	shoe	shovel	washer

a)  ____________

b)  ____________

c)  ____________

d) 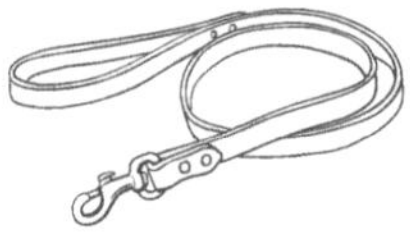 ____________

e)  ____________

f)  ____________

g) 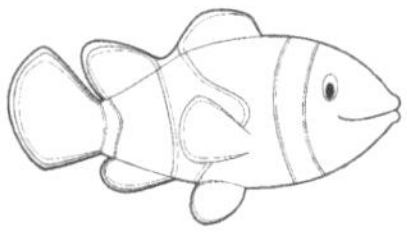 ____________

h)  ____________

i)  ____________

j)  ____________

Brain Stretch

- Create a word search puzzle based on the words above.
- On a piece of paper, write a sentence using each word.

Words with *sh* (cont.)

2. Fill in the blank with the correct ***sh*** word.

a) I put a ________________ on my dog.

b) Mom uses a ________________ to dig in the dirt.

c) I like to catch ________________ with my dad.

d) Jack puts on his ________________ to go outside.

e) Linda has some ________________ to buy a toy.

f) ________________ have sharp teeth.

g) Dad puts our dirty clothes in the ________________.

h) We keep our garden tools in the ________________.

i) A ________________ is a very big boat.

j) Some birds made a nest in that ________________.

bush
cash
fish
leash
sharks
shed
ship
shoes
shovel
washer

Unit 5

Words with *ck*

1 Say each word out loud. Look at where a ***ck*** sound can be in a word. Write the correct word beside the picture.

bucket	clock	duck	jacket	kick
lock	rocket	sock	stick	truck

a)  ____________

b)  ____________

c)  ____________

d)  ____________

e)  ____________

f)  ____________

g)  ____________

h)  ____________

i)  ____________

j)  ____________

Brain Stretch

- Create a word search puzzle based on the words above.
- On a piece of paper, write a sentence using each word.

Words with ck (cont.)

2 Fill in the blank with the correct ***ck*** word.

a) A ________________ is swimming in the pond.

b) My friends and I ________________ the ball.

c) Granny checks the time on a ________________.

d) Jim's new puppy chewed up his ________________.

e) The ________________ is filled with water.

f) My dad drives a big ________________ for work.

g) I use a ________________ to keep my bike safe.

h) Our dog plays fetch with a ________________.

i) A ________________ took off for outer space.

j) When I'm cold, I put on a ________________.

bucket
clock
duck
jacket
kick
lock
rocket
sock
stick
truck

Unit 6

Words with *th* and *wh*

1. Say each word out loud.
   Listen to the sounds the letters *th* and *wh* make.
   Sort the *th* and *wh* words. Write them into the chart.

both	father	moth	nowhere	pinwheel
third	thumb	wheat	when	why

th words	*wh* words
__________	__________
__________	__________
__________	__________
__________	__________
__________	__________

2. Write a sentence using a word from each list.

____

____

Words with *th* and *wh* (cont.)

3 Say the name of the object out loud.

Write the letters ***th*** or ***wh*** to complete the word.

a) 

_____ale

b) 

_____umb

c) 

_____istle

d) 

_____eel

e) 

Ear_____

f) 

ba_____

4 Fill in the blank using the best word from the list.

three	tooth	where	who

a) I think I have a loose ______________.

b) ______________ left the door open?

c) My sister is turning ______________ today.

d) ______________ did you put my backpack?

Unit 7

Words with *ch* and *tch*

1. Say each word out loud.
Listen to the sounds the letters *ch* and *tch* make.
Sort the *ch* and *tch* words. Write them into the chart.

chin	chop	couch	fetch	hatch
itch	much	patch	pitch	which

ch words	*tch* words
___________	___________
___________	___________
___________	___________
___________	___________
___________	___________

2. Write a sentence using a word from each list.

____

____

Words with *ch* and *tch* (cont.)

3 Say the name of the object out loud.

Write the letters ***ch*** or ***tch*** to complete the word.

a) 

wa______

b) 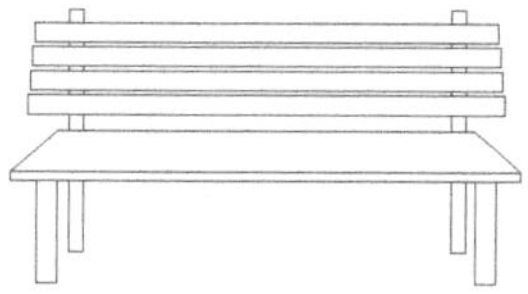

ben______

c) 

______ain

d) 

wi______

e) 

______air

f) 

ma______

4 Fill in the blank using the best word from the list.

catch	ketchup	lunch	March

a) I like to play ________________ outside with my dad.

b) ________________ is my favourite meal of the day.

c) I like to put ________________ on my hot dog.

d) My birthday is in ________________.

Unit 8

Short and Long Vowels

Long vowels say their name. **Short vowels** make different sounds. Read the examples below. Say the names of the objects out loud.

a

short ă  jam

long ā 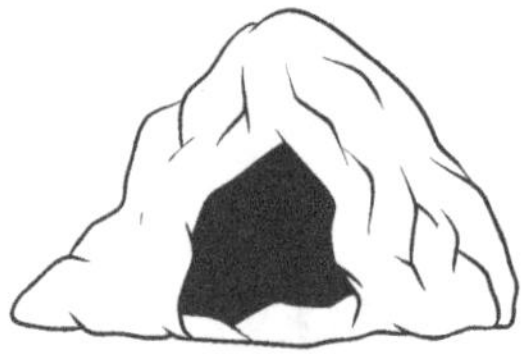 cave

e

short ĕ 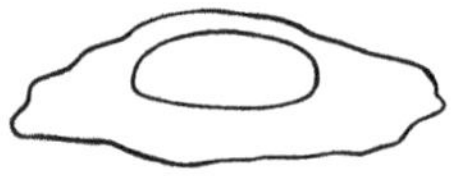 egg

long ē  leaf

i

short ĭ 

milk

long ī 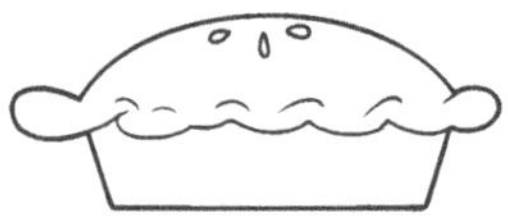 pie

o

short ŏ  top

long ō  globe

u

short ŭ  nut

long ū 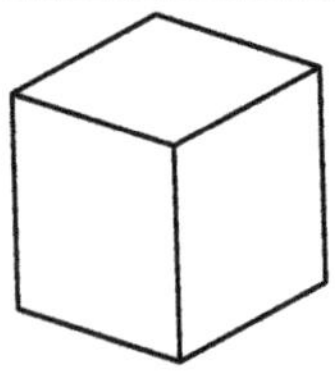 cube

Short Vowels

1 Fill in the missing vowel. Colour the pictures.

a) 

f____n

b) 

l____ck

c) 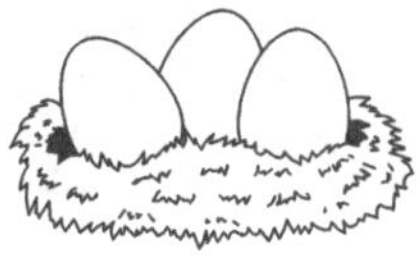

n____st

d) 

f____sh

e) 

dr____m

f) 

b____t

g) 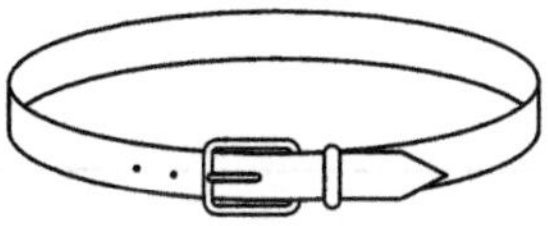

b____lt

h) 

t____p

i) 

dr____ll

j) 

n____t

k) 

j____m

l) 

b____ll

Colour the short *a* words. red
Colour the short *e* words. blue
Colour the short *i* words. green
Colour the short *o* words. yellow
Colour the short *u* words. purple

Short Vowels (cont.)

2 Fill in the missing vowel. Colour the pictures.

a) 

n____t

b) 

p____g

c) 

d____ll

d) 

t____b

e) 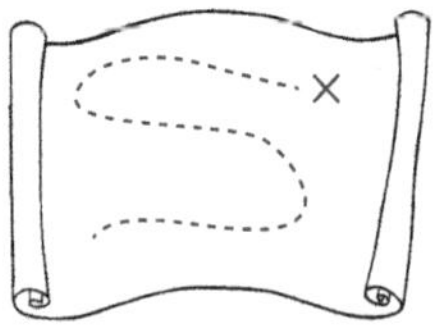

m____p

f) 

p____n

3 Fill in the blank using the best word from the list.

bug	cup	hat	net	pen

a) I need a ____________ to write my name.

b) The little ____________ crawled up the wall.

c) The fish was caught in a ____________ in the lake.

d) I wear a ____________ to keep the sun out of my eyes.

e) I drank water from a ____________ this morning.

Short Vowels (cont.)

4 Write each word in the correct box.

and	best	bill	fun	hot
hug	job	red	sat	sip
stop	up	win	yes	zap

short *a*	short *e*	short *i*	short *o*	short *u*
______	______	______	______	______
______	______	______	______	______
______	______	______	______	______

5 Write the word from the list that rhymes with the word below.

a) tap ________________ b) vest ________________

c) rug ________________ d) spill ________________

e) shed ________________ f) bob ________________

Long Vowels

1 Fill in the missing vowel. Colour the pictures.

a)

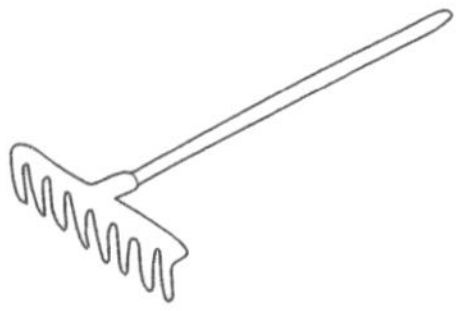

r_____ke

b)

b_____ak

c)

men_____

d)

d_____ce

e)

ph_____ne

f)

s_____al

g)

f_____re

h)

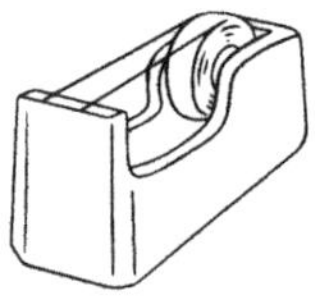

t_____pe

i)

n_____te

j)

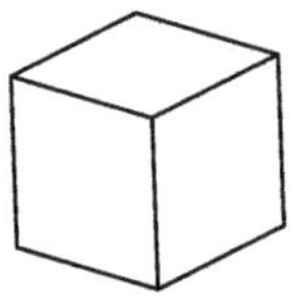

c_____be

k)

tr_____e

l)

d_____me

Colour the long *a* words. red

Colour the long *e* words. blue

Colour the long *i* words. green

Colour the long *o* words. yellow

Colour the long *u* words. purple

Long Vowels (cont.)

2 Fill in the missing vowel. Colour the pictures.

a) 

_____nicorn

b) 

sh_____ep

c) 

b_____wl

d) 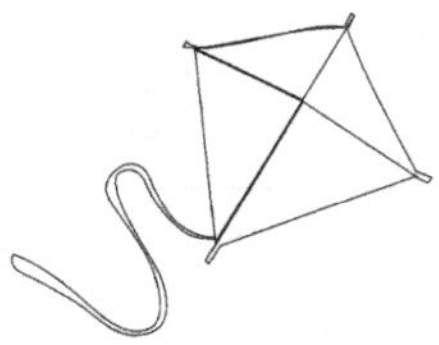

k_____te

e) 

k_____y

f) 

sn_____ke

3 Fill in the blank using the best word from the list.

bite	cake	cube	kite	Pete	use

a) A _______________ is a six-sided object.

b) My friend's name is _______________ and he has a pet dog.

c) I like to fly a _______________ on a windy day.

d) Ana had a vanilla _______________ for her birthday.

e) The mosquito gave me a _______________ on my arm.

f) I can _______________ my new umbrella next time it rains.

Long Vowels (cont.)

4 Write each word in the correct box.

baby	cone	feel	here	hide
hole	home	huge	late	mule
neat	pipe	time	unit	wave

long *a*	long *e*	long *i*	long *o*	long *u*
______	______	______	______	______
______	______	______	______	______
______	______	______	______	______

5 Write the word from the list that rhymes with the word below.

a) brave ______________ b) gate ______________

c) wide ______________ d) mole ______________

e) wheel ______________ f) seat ______________

Short and Long Vowels

Colour the **long vowel** words. red

Colour the **short vowel** words. blue

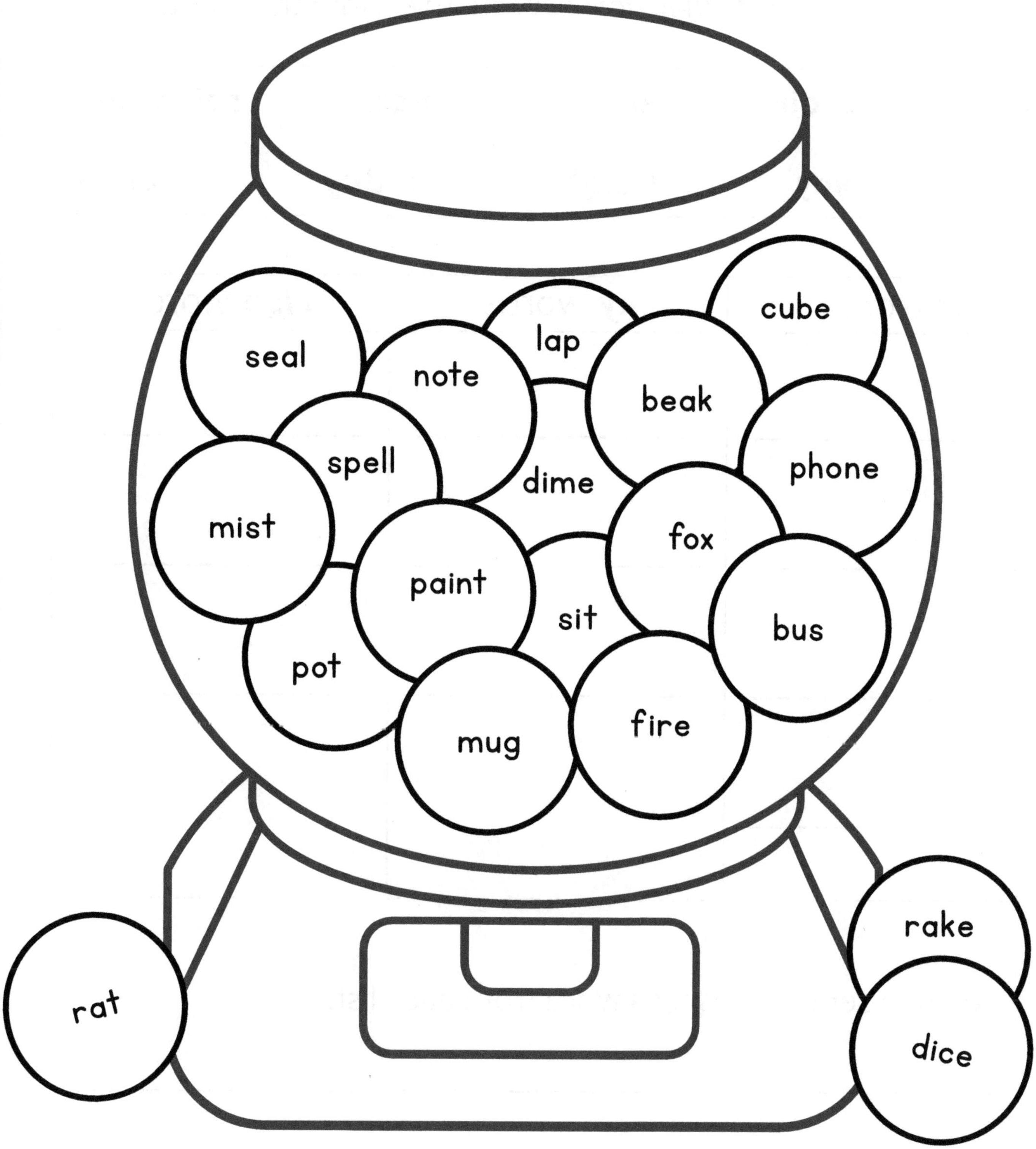

Unit 9

Words with *ai*, *ay*, and *eigh*

1. Say each word out loud.
Listen to the long ***a*** sound the letters *ai*, *ay*, and ***eigh*** make.
Sort the *ai*, *ay*, and ***eigh*** words. Write them into the chart.

bay	brain	drain	main	neighbour
sail	say	sleigh	today	weight

ai words	***ay*** words	***eigh*** words
____________	____________	____________
____________	____________	____________
____________	____________	____________
____________		

2. Write a sentence using a word from each list.

____

____

Words with *ai, ay, and eigh* (cont.)

3. Fill in the blank using the best word from the list.

clay	holiday	nail
paint	play	tail

a) Hamed and I ________________ a game of Go Fish.

b) Kate wants to ________________ a picture of a cat.

c) Thanksgiving is John's favourite ________________.

d) My dad uses a ________________ to fix the shelf.

e) I made a sculpture out of ________________.

f) Our dog wags his ________________ when he's happy.

4. Say the name of the object out loud.
Write the letters *ai, ay,* and ***eigh*** to complete the word.

a)

tr_____n

b)

_____t

c)

spr_____

Unit 10 Words with *au* and *aw*

1. Say each word out loud.
   Listen to the sounds the letters *au* and *aw* make.
   Sort the *au* and *aw* words. Write them into the chart.

audio	author	dawn	draw	haunt
launch	lawn	raw	taught	yawn

au words	*aw* words
____________	____________
____________	____________
____________	____________
____________	____________
____________	____________

2. Write a sentence using a word from each list.

____

____

Words with *au* and *aw* (cont.)

3 Say the name of the object out loud.

Write the letters ***au*** or ***aw*** to complete the word.

a) 

f______cet

b) 

p______

c) 

______tumn

d) 

str______

e) 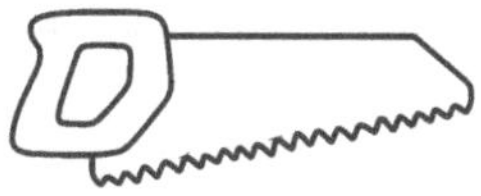

s______

f) 

l______ndry

4 Fill in the blank using the best word from the list.

August	crawl	sauce	yawn

a) My mom cooked a pot of spaghetti ________________.

b) My baby cousin is just starting to ________________.

c) When I'm tired, I ________________.

d) My dad's birthday is in ________________.

Unit 11 Words with ee, ea, and ey

1. Say each word out loud.
Listen to the long ***e*** sound the letters ***ee, ea,*** and ***ey*** make.
Sort the ***ee, ea,*** and ***ey*** words. Write them into the chart.

cheese	dream	each	freeze	honey
monkey	peel	tea	tree	turkey

ee words	***ea*** words	***ey*** words
__________	__________	__________
__________	__________	__________
__________	__________	__________
__________		

2. Write a sentence using a word from each list.

____

____

Words with ee, ea, and ey (cont.)

3 Fill in the blank using the best word from the list.

meal	read	seed
steal	teeth	week

a) I planted a ________________ in the garden.

b) Friday is Jay's favourite day of the ________________.

c) Our puppy tries to ________________ food off the table.

d) Before bed, Tessa likes to ________________ her book.

e) After breakfast, Han brushes his ________________.

f) Dinner is my favourite ________________ of the day.

4 Say the name of the object out loud.
Write the letters *ee*, *ea*, and *ey* to complete the word.

a)

sh_____p

b)

b_____ch

c)

monk_____

Unit 12

Words with *ie* and *igh*

1 Say each word out loud.
Listen to the sound the letters ***ie*** and ***igh*** make.
Sort the ***ie*** and ***igh*** words. Write them into the chart.

bright	die	flies	fries
high	night	sight	tie

ie words	***igh*** words
________	________
________	________
________	________
________	________

2 Write a sentence using a word from each list.

____

____

Words with *ie* and *igh* (cont.)

3 Fill in the blank using the best word from the list.

flies	fried	knight
light	right	tie

a) I need to ______________ my shoes before I go play.

b) We had yummy ______________ chicken for dinner.

c) You're ______________! You got it!

d) So many ______________ are flying around the trash can.

e) The ______________ wore shiny armour.

f) Turn on the ______________ when it gets dark outside.

4 Say the name of the object out loud.
Write the letters ***ie*** or ***igh*** to complete the word.

a) 

t_____

b) 

d_____

c) 

l_____t

Unit 13

Words with y as Long *i* and Long *e* Sounds

1 Say each word out loud. Sort the ***y as long i*** and ***y as long e*** words. Write them into the chart.

bunny	buy	jelly	lily	my
rainy	sky	try	very	why

y as long i words	***y as long e*** words
____________	____________
____________	____________
____________	____________
____________	____________
____________	____________

2 Unscramble the word. Write the word to fill in the blank.

a) It is very cold and ______________ outside. (**yiarn**)

b) Birds can ______________ very fast. (**lyf**)

c) I earned ______________ for doing my chores. (**menoy**)

Words with y as Long *i* and Long e Sounds (cont.)

3 Each word below has one of the two ***y*** sounds.

Circle the correct answer for each word.

a) 

Long ē

Long ī

b) 

Long ē

Long ī

c) 

Long ē

Long ī

d) 

Long ē

Long ī

e) 

Long ē

Long ī

f) 

Long ē

Long ī

g) 

Long ē

Long ī

h) 

Long ē

Long ī

i) 

Long ē

Long ī

j) 

Long ē

Long ī

k) 

Long ē

Long ī

l) 

Long ē

Long ī

Colour the y *as long i* words. yellow

Colour the y *as long e* words. green

Unit 14 Words with *oa*, *oe*, and *ow*

1 Say each word out loud.
Listen to the long ***o*** sound the letters ***oa***, ***oe***, and ***ow*** make.
Sort the ***oa***, ***oe***, and ***ow*** words. Write them into the chart.

below	crow	doe	foe	follow
goal	grow	oak	toad	toe

oa words	***ow*** words	***oe*** words

2 Write a sentence using a word from each list.

____

____

Words with *oa*, *oe*, and *ow* (cont.)

3. Fill in the blank using the best word from the list.

blows	glow	hoe
throat	toast	yellow

a) For breakfast, I have jam on my ________________.

b) Grandma loves the colour ________________.

c) Becky's new sneakers ________________ in the dark.

d) When Tom's soup is hot, he ________________ on it.

e) My ________________ hurts, so I might be getting sick.

f) Mom uses a ________________ in the garden.

4. Say the name of the object out loud.
Write the letters ***oa***, ***oe***, or ***ow*** to complete the word.

a)

c______t

b)
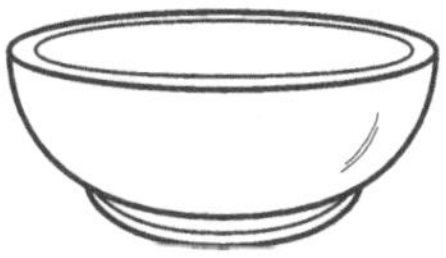
b______l

c)

t______

Unit 15

Words with *ui*, *ue*, and *ew*

1 Say each word out loud.

Listen to the sound the letters ***ui***, ***ue***, and ***ew*** make.

Sort the ***ui***, ***ue***, and ***ew*** words. Write them into the chart.

blue	due	fruit	glue	juice
knew	stew	suit	threw	

ui words	***ue*** words	***ew*** words
______	______	______
______	______	______
______	______	______

2 Write two words from the list that rhyme with the word below.

a) clue ______ ______

b) new ______ ______

Words with *ui*, *ue*, and *ew* (cont.)

3 Fill in the blank using the best word from the list.

blew	bruise	drew
due	statue	suit

a) I have an assignment ______________ tomorrow.

b) On my birthday, I ______________ out the candles.

c) At the museum, there was a big ______________.

d) I ______________ a picture in my sketchbook.

e) I fell and got a ______________ on my knee.

f) My dad wore a ______________ for his work meeting.

4 Say the name of the object out loud.
Write the letters ***ui***, ***ue***, or ***ew*** to complete the word.

a)

fr_____t

b)
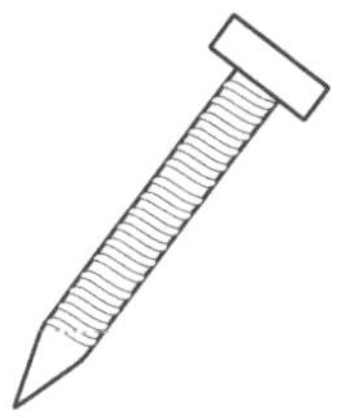
scr_____

c)

tiss_____

Unit 16 Words with Silent e

1 Say the name of the object out loud. Circle the correct word. Colour the picture.

a)

bat bate

b)

tub tube

c)

can cane

d)

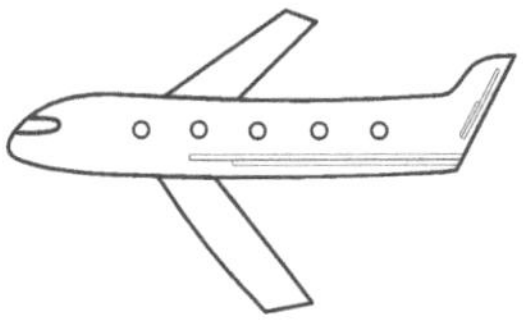

plane plan

e)

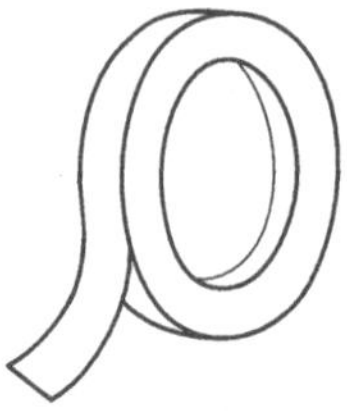

tape tap

f)

kit kite

g)

hate hat

h)

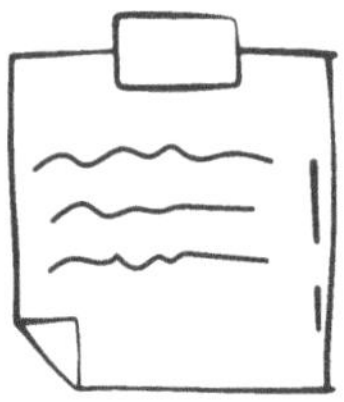

note not

i)

huge hug

j)

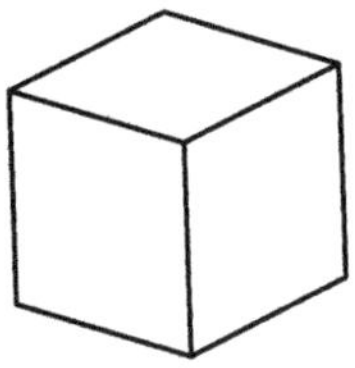

cube cub

k)

car care

l)

made mad

Words with Silent e (cont.)

2 Read the sentence.
Fill in the blank with the correct word for the sentence.

a) My new kitten is very small and _______________.
(cut cute)

b) Thomas is wearing a blue _______________.
(hat hate)

c) I picked up the _______________ of toothpaste.
(tub tube)

d) I _______________ my friend is at school today.
(hop hope)

e) There are lots of people _______________ the concert.
(at ate)

f) My mom opened a _______________ of soup for lunch.
(can cane)

g) I _______________ a new friend at soccer practice.
(mad made)

Unit 17

Words with *ar* and *or*

1 Say each word out loud. Write the correct word beside the picture.

barn	car	corn	forest	fork
park	shark	shorts	star	storm

a)  ____________________

b)  ____________________

c)  ____________________

d) 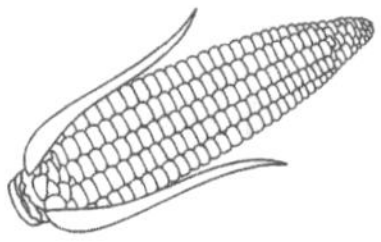 ____________________

e)  ____________________

f)  ____________________

g)  ____________________

h)  ____________________

i)  ____________________

j)  ____________________

Colour the *ar* words. orange   Colour the short *or* words. purple

Words with *ar* and *or* (cont.)

2 Say the name of the object out loud.
Fill in the blank with ***ar*** or ***or*** to complete the word.

a)

h______p

b)

h______se

c)

j______

d)
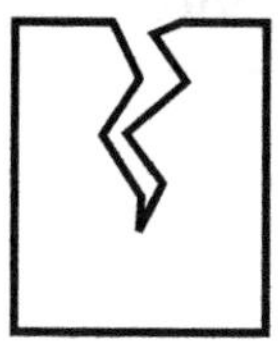
t______n

e)

ac______n

f)

y______n

3 Fill in the blank using the best word from the list.

card	far	horn	horse

a) Jack ran really ______________ in gym class today.

b) I made my mom a ______________ for her birthday.

c) Lin rode a ______________ at the barn today.

d) My dad honked the car ______________.

Unit 18 Words with *er*, *ir*, and *ur*

1. Say each word out loud.
   Listen to the sounds the letters *er*, *ir*, and *ur* make.
   Sort the *er*, *ir*, and *ur* words. Write them into the chart.

burn	circus	curl	dirt	first	hurt
nurse	otter	river	serve	stir	water

er words	*ir* words	*ur* words
______	______	______
______	______	______
______	______	______
______	______	______

2. Write a sentence using a word from each list.

____

____

Words with *er*, *ir*, and *ur* (cont.)

3. Say the name of the object out loud.

Write the letters ***er***, ***ir***, or ***ur*** to complete the word.

a)  p______se	b)  lett______	c)  sh______t
d)  flow______	e)  s______f	f)  b______d
g)  t______tle	h) 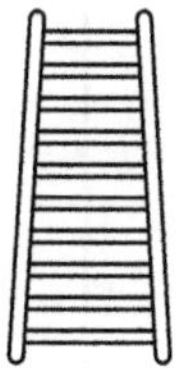 ladd______	i) 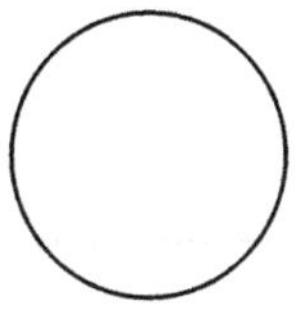 c______cle
j)  tig______	k)  sk______t	l)  t______n

Colour the *er* words. purple Colour the *ir* words. green

Colour the *ur* words. blue

Unit 19

Words with *oi* and *oy*

1 Say each word out loud.
Listen to the sounds the letters *oi* and *oy* make.
Sort the *oi* and *oy* words. Write them into the chart.

annoy	choice	enjoy	noise	point
royal	soy	spoil	toy	voice

oi words	*oy* words
______	______
______	______
______	______
______	______
______	______

2 Write a sentence using a word from each list.

____

____

Words with *oi* and *oy* (cont.)

3. Say the name of the object out loud.

   Write the letters ***oi*** or ***oy*** to complete the word.

a) 

c______n

b) 

t______

c) 

s______l

d) 

b______

e) 

cowb______

f) 

t______let

4. Fill in the blank using the best word from the list.

destroy	loyal	noisy	oil

a) When Todd cooks, he uses a lot of ______________.

b) My dog is ______________ and follows me everywhere.

c) It is very ______________ at the theme park.

d) We built a block tower, then got to ______________ it.

Unit 20

Words with *ou* and *ow*

1. Say each word out loud.
   Listen to the sounds the letters *ou* and *ow* make.
   Sort the *ou* and *ow* words. Write them into the chart.

about	count	down	frown	hour
how	howl	shout	sour	town

ou words	*ow* words
______________	______________
______________	______________
______________	______________
______________	______________
______________	______________

2. Write a sentence using a word from each list.

____

____

Words with *ou* and *ow* (cont.)

3. Say the name of the object out loud.

   Write the letters ***ou*** or ***ow*** to complete the word.

a) 

cl_____n

b) 

m_____se

c) 

cr_____n

d) 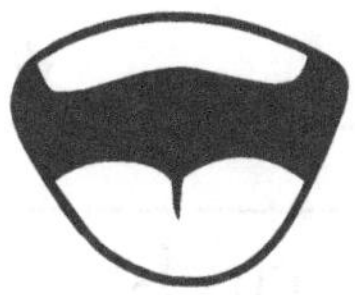

m_____th

e) 

cl_____d

f) 

fl_____er

g) 

t_____el

h) 

c_____

i) 

h_____se

j) 

o_____

k) 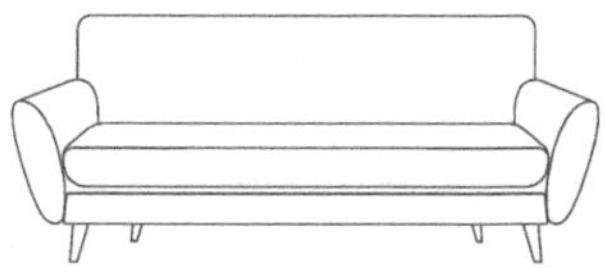

c_____ch

l) 

m_____ntain

Colour the *ou* words. yellow　　Colour the *ow* words. pink

Unit 21

Words with Long *oo* and Short *oo* Sounds

The letters *oo* can have the ***short oo*** sound, like in **book**.
The letters *oo* can have the ***long oo*** sound, like in **moon**.

1 Say each word out loud.
Listen to the sounds the *oo* make.
Sort the *short oo* and *long oo* words. Write them into the chart.

cook	food	foot	hook
moon	pool	tooth	wood

short *oo* words	long *oo* words
______________	______________
______________	______________
______________	______________
______________	______________

2 Write a sentence using a word from each list.

____

____

Words with Long oo and Short oo Sounds (cont.)

3. Fill in the blank using the best word from the list.

choose	good	look
spoon	stool	took

a) Amy uses a ________________ to eat the soup.

b) I ________________ the bus to school today.

c) ________________ a candy from the bowl.

d) ________________ at all the clouds in the sky.

e) At the counter, I sit on a ________________.

f) I hope you have a ________________ day.

4. Colour the ***short oo*** words. red

Colour the ***long oo*** words. yellow

a)

b)

c)

Unit 22

Phonics Review

Long a

ai	ay	eigh	a_e
	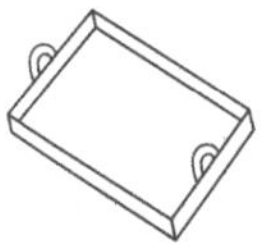		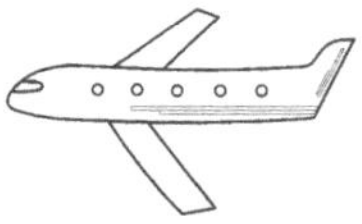
snail	tray	eight	plane

Long e

ea	ee	ey	e_e

leaf	bee	turkey	athlete

Long i

ie	igh	y	i_e
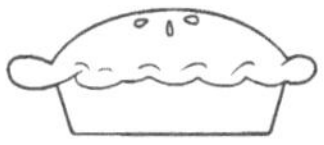			
pie	light	fly	bike

Long o

oa	ow	oe	o_e
			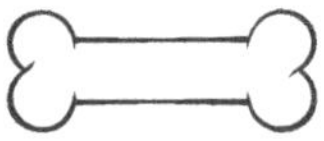
coat	crow	toe	bone

Long u

ue	ui	ew	u_e
			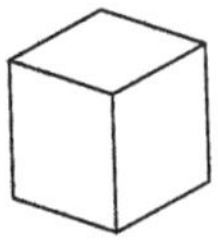
tissue	juice	jewel	cube

Phonics Review

1 Say the name of the object out loud.
Fill in the missing letters for the word. Colour the pictures.

a) ow ou

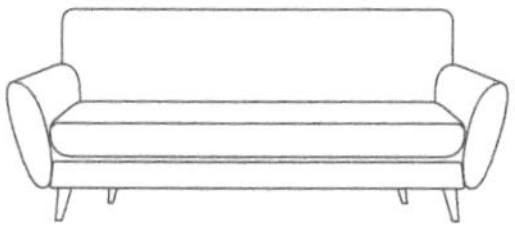

c_____ch

b) y igh

l_____t

c) ea ee

l_____f

d) ui ew

fr_____t

e) ar or

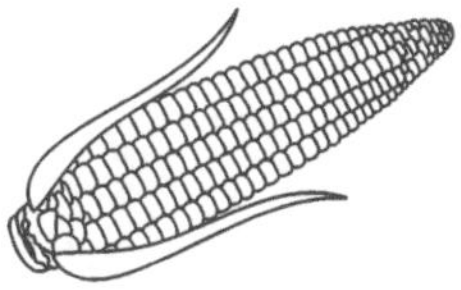

c_____n

f) ee ey

turk_____

g) ir er

f_____st

h) ur er

b_____n

i) ew ue

tiss_____

j) ur ir

b_____d

k) aw au

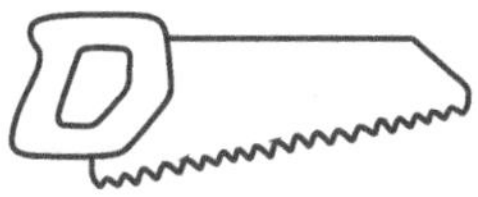

s_____

l) oy oi

c_____n

Phonics Review (cont.)

2 Say the name of the object out loud.
Fill in the missing letters for the word. Colour the pictures.

a) ey ea

monk______

b) or ar

h______p

c) ay eigh

______t

d) er ir

tig______

e) ir er

sh______t

f) ow oe

t______

g) aw au

f______cet

h) ou oa

m______se

i) ew ui

j______ce

j) ee ea

st______m

k) ar or

b______n

l) aw au

______tumn

Phonics Review (cont.)

3 Say the name of the object out loud.
Fill in the missing letters for the word. Colour the pictures.

a) oa ow

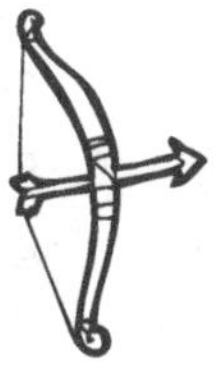

b____

b) aw au

p____

c) ew ue

j____el

d) igh ie

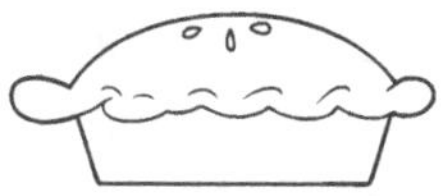

p____

e) ee ea

tr____

f) or ar

sh____k

g) ay eigh

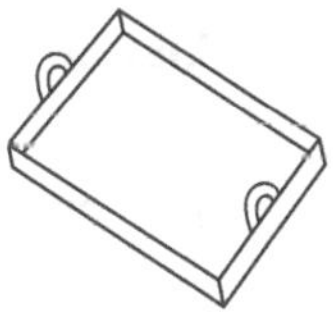

tr____

h) oa ow

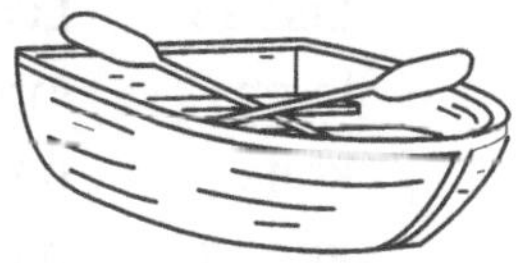

b____t

i) ee ea

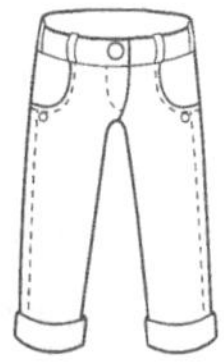

j____ns

j) igh ie

d____

k) ui eu

s____t

l) eigh ai

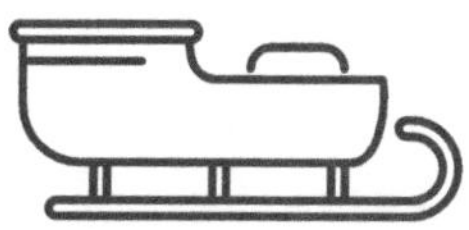

sl____

Spelling Word List

List 1	List 2	List 3	List 4	List 5	List 6	List 7	List 8	List 9	List 10
cap	his	onto	up	red	save	keep	pie	cry	road
had	him	hot	bus	leg	page	dream	tight	baby	snow
and	if	dog	hug	tell	today	eat	kind	try	hope
sat	big	cob	run	yes	wait	three	time	any	also
pan	pin	box	us	went	stay	easy	night	only	glow
lap	fix	off	but	bed	sale	need	bite	why	goal
jam	will	stop	cut	let	play	meet	write	many	throw
hat	win	lost	fun	wet	rain	read	high	story	soap
yam	dig	fog	must	end	game	each	right	very	nose
can	pit	job	jug	best	take	mean	pine	fly	follow

List 11	List 12	List 13	List 14	List 15	List 16	List 17	List 18	List 19	List 20
book	bark	skip	from	push	sock	which	chin	plus	cube
took	party	smart	crab	trash	quack	what	witch	race	few
food	yard	just	drip	dish	luck	there	much	toss	huge
cook	barn	still	brush	shake	pick	where	catch	ice	mule
clue	farm	snack	bring	wish	clock	both	chat	sip	yew
school	hard	smell	grab	share	neck	who	lunch	once	you
threw	star	spill	trip	fresh	pack	that	chick	miss	use
crew	dark	swim	pretty	shell	deck	when	itch	nice	fuel
soon	card	scarf	tree	washer	rock	this	watch	same	chew
should	mark	slip	frog	brush	flick	those	match	circle	cue

List 21	List 22	List 23	List 24	List 25	List 26	List 27	List 28
join	how	pause	rose	lamb	into	girl	middle
boy	found	straw	pace	knife	backpack	burn	soccer
oil	sour	sauce	hike	gnome	bathtub	first	buzz
coin	about	hawk	tale	night	sunset	dirt	silly
loyal	town	cause	scene	calm	inside	fur	apple
toy	shout	hall	whale	hour	birthday	curl	bottle
noise	now	raw	ripe	sign	today	bird	little
enjoy	down	boss	game	walk	cupcake	hurt	bubble
foil	hour	draw	note	write	bedtime	birth	grass
royal	loud	doll	shape	ghost	fireman	turn	button

Try writing a funny sentence using the words from each spelling word list.

Ideas to Practice Spelling Words

Colour Code

Write out your spelling words using one colour for the vowels and another colour for the consonants.

Rainbow Words

Write out your spelling words into the shape of a rainbow using the colours of the rainbow.

Hidden Words

Draw a picture outline. Add your spelling words to the picture so they are "hiding." Colour your picture.

Cut It Out!

Cut letters out of a magazine. Use the letters to spell out your words. Glue them onto a sheet of paper.

Word Search

Create a word search based on your spelling words.

Rhyming Words

Write out your spelling words. Write a rhyming word next to each spelling word.

Alphabetical Order

Print your spelling words in alphabetical order.

Spelling Word Typing

Type your spelling words on a computer or other device.

Magnetic Letter Words

Use magnetic letters to make your spelling words.

Spelling Race

How many times can you write out your spelling words in three minutes?

Sort It Out

Sort your spelling words into categories of your choice. Record them on a piece of paper.

Spelling Word Fun

Form your spelling words using

- modelling clay
- pipe cleaners
- toothpicks

What Is a Sentence?

A **sentence** is a group of words that tells a complete idea.

A **sentence** always begins with a **capital letter**.

✓ This is a sentence: **The dog runs fast.**

✗ This is not a sentence: **Fast dog.**

1 Use a ✓ to mark the groups of words that are a sentence.
Use an ✗ to mark the groups of words that are not a sentence.

a) A new car. ________

b) My dog runs. ________

c) The fish can swim. ________

d) The song. ________

e) The little boy waved. ________

f) My question. ________

2 Add words to make a complete sentence.

a) The pretty bird ______________________________.

b) The loud car ______________________________.

c) The big tree ______________________________.

d) Ryan and Lacey ______________________________.

e) ______________________________ ate a snack.

Exploring Kinds of Sentences

. A **telling** sentence ends with a **period**.
Examples: I have a pet. We are going to the park.

? An **asking** sentence ends with a **question mark**.
Examples: Do you have a pet? Is it a dog?

! An **exclamation** sentence shows a **strong feeling** or **excitement** and ends with an **exclamation mark**.
Examples: I love my pet! Wow! Ouch!

! . A **command** sentence tells someone to do something. It can end with a **period** or with an **exclamation mark**.
Examples: Feed your pet. Watch out!

1. Write a **telling** sentence.

____

2. Write an **asking** sentence.

____

3. Write a sentence that shows **excitement**.

____

4. Write a **command** sentence.

____

Exploring Kinds of Sentences (cont.)

5 Write the correct punctuation at the end of each sentence.

a)  Do you want a slice of pizza ☐

b) Take off your wet shoes ☐ 

c)  Yuck ☐

d) What is your name ☐ 

e)  I love this movie ☐

f) Wash your hands ☐ 

g)  When is your birthday ☐

Making a Noun Collage

A **noun** is a word that names a person, place, or thing.

Create a **noun** collage.

Cut out pictures from magazines or flyers that represent nouns.

Glue them into the correct category.

People
Places
Things

What Is a Noun?

A **noun** is a word that names a person, place, or thing.

1. Name a noun that is a **person**. ______________________________

2. Name a noun that is a **place**. ______________________________

3. Name a noun that is a **thing**. ______________________________

4. Underline the **nouns** in the sentence. The first one is done for you.

   a) <u>Halifax</u> is a <u>Canadian</u> city.

   b) The girl and her mother walked the dog.

   c) I drew a picture using crayons and markers.

   d) She got some very nice flowers from the garden.

   e) His favourite shoes have blue laces.

   f) Hotdogs and hamburgers are my favourite lunches.

Nouns: Am I a Person, Place, or Thing?

Colour the **people**. red

Colour the **places**. blue

Colour the **things**. green

library	boy	arcade	book
fork	pencil	dog	teacher
mayor	toy	store	student
farm	bread	park	nurse

Plural Nouns

A **plural noun** names more than one person, place, or thing.
Add **s** to most nouns to make them plural.
*Example: log ⟶ **logs***

1 Write the plural form for each **noun** by adding **s**.

a) pig ________________ b) train ________________

c) jar ________________ d) snack ________________

e) crayon ________________ f) drum ________________

Some **nouns** use a new word to name **more than one**.
*Example: man ⟶ **men***

2 Match the correct word to name more than one.

foot •	• geese
goose •	• women
woman •	• feet

Plural Nouns (cont.)

A **plural noun** names **more than one** person, place, or thing.

Add **es** to nouns that end with ***sh***, ***ch***, ***x***, or ***s***.

Examples: *brush* ⟶ ***brushes***

watch ⟶ ***watches***

mix ⟶ ***mixes***

glass ⟶ ***glasses***

3 Write the plural for each **noun** by adding ***s*** or ***es***.

a) fox________ b) ruler________

c) cat________ d) beach________

e) class________ f) backpack________

g) mug________ h) box________

i) bus________ j) dress________

Pronouns: *me, you, her, him, us, them, it*

A **pronoun** is a word that replaces a noun.
We can use pronouns to replace the object of a sentence.

Example pronouns are: **me, you, her, him, us, them, it**.

1 Rewrite the sentence. Replace the underlined word or words with the correct **pronoun**. Use the word box to help you.

him	she	us

a) Samantha walked to the mall with Matthew.

____.

b) My mom waited for me and my brother.

____.

Pronouns: *me, you, her, him, us, them, it* (cont.)

2 Read the pair of sentences.
Circle the **pronoun** in the second sentence of each pair.
Write what the **pronoun** stands for.

a) Sarah likes to play soccer. She is on a team.

Stands for: ______________________________

b) Buster barked at the mail carrier. He was very loud.

Stands for: ______________________________

c) Jack and Jill went up the hill. They were looking for water.

Stands for: ______________________________

d) The ice cream was left outside. It melted in the hot sun.

Stands for: ______________________________

e) Tim and I went to the park. We had a great time.

Stands for: ______________________________

Proper Nouns Need a Capital Letter

Nouns that always begin with a capital letter are called **proper nouns**.

The names of **people** and **pets** begin with a capital letter.

Dr. Hill John Ms. Chang Mrs. Jones

Fluffy Sara Mr. Smith Benji

The names of **specific places** begin with a capital letter.

Canada Oak Road Adams Park

Vancouver Ontario Carling Arena

Days of the week and **months** begin with a capital letter.

May Monday Friday March

November Thursday July Saturday

Holidays and **special days** begin with a capital letter.

Canada Day Remembrance Day Labour Day

Halloween Thanksgiving Family Day

Proper Nouns

1 Use **proper nouns** to complete the sentence.

a) My friend's name is ______________________________.

b) My favourite holiday is ______________________________.

c) My birthday month is ______________________________.

d) I live in the province of ______________________________.

2 Identify the proper nouns.

- Circle the names of **people** and **pets**. red
- Circle **specific places**. blue
- Circle names of **weekdays** or **months**. green
- Circle **holidays** and **special days**. yellow

Stacey	Canada	Fido	Thursday
March	Tristan	Oakville Mall	Christmas
New Year's Day	Monday	Valentine's Day	Toronto

Nouns: Compound Words

A **compound word** is a word that is made up of two or more words.

Match the words in the same shapes to create a **compound word**.

1 back — fly

2 butter — plane

3 week — pack

4 air — end

Nouns: Compound Word Challenge

Use the words to make as many **compound words** as you can.

back	pan	dog	beach
box	cup	gold	bow
ball	pack	fire	jelly
cake	fly	sand	rain
mail	tooth	castle	brush
snow	fish	man	house

Making a Verb Collage

A **verb** is an action word that tells what happens.

Every sentence has a verb.

*Example: The boy **runs** fast.* ⟶ The action word is ***runs***.

Cut out pictures from magazines and flyers that represent **verbs**. Paste them into the box below.

Verbs: Simple Present Tense

A **verb** is an action word that shows what someone or something is doing.

For example, "run," "jump," and "swim" are all verbs because they describe actions.

1 Circle the **verb** in the sentence. Print the **verb** on the line.

a) The cat sits on the mat. ____________________

b) I jump on the bed. ____________________

c) The sun shines in the sky. ____________________

d) Mom hugs me tight. ____________________

2 Write a sentence about the picture. Use an action **verb** and circle it.

____

Present Tense Verb: "To Be"

The verb "**to be**" helps us talk about who or what someone or something is. Here are the words we use:

I am	**It is**
You are	**We are**
He/She is	**They are**

1 Fill in the blank with the correct word from the word box.

are	am	is

a) I ___________ happy.

b) You ___________ funny.

c) She ___________ kind.

d) It ___________ a cat.

e) They ___________ tall.

f) We ___________ seven.

2 Colour the image below. Write a sentence for the image using the verb "**to be.**" Use the learning box to help you.

a)  ____

b)  ____

Past Tense Verb: "To Be"

The past tense of the verb "**to be**" tells us what something was like or where someone or something was in the past.

I was happy yesterday.

The cat and the dog were playing together yesterday.

1 Fill in the blank with the correct word from the word box.

was	were

a) The sun ___________ hot.

b) The flowers ___________ blue.

c) They ___________ happy.

d) He ___________ tired.

e) The car ___________ red.

f) We ___________ at the beach.

2 Colour the image below. Write a sentence for the image using the past tense of the verb "**to be.**" Use the learning box to help you.

a)  ____

b)  ____

Verbs: Using the Past Tense

A **past tense** verb tells about something that has already happened.

Add an ***ed*** to make the past tense.

*Example: Yesterday, I **walked** to school.*

If a verb ends with a silent ***e***, add a ***d*** to make it past tense.

*Example: Last Saturday, I **baked** a cake.*

Fill in the blanks by adding ***d*** or ***ed*** to make the verbs **past tense**.

1. Last night, my grandma ________________ me.
   call

2. I ________________ at my birthday party.
   dance

3. Last summer, we ________________ at the beach.
   play

4. Sofia ________________ the leaves last weekend.
   rake

5. Yesterday, you ________________ me find my lost keys.
   help

6. Peter and Omar ________________ their hands before dinner.
   wash

Verbs: Irregular Past Tense

Irregular verbs are verbs that don't follow the regular pattern of adding ***ed*** to make the past tense.

1 Use the word box to fill in the correct **past tense** verb.

fell	left	ran	rode

a)  ____________________ fall

b)  ____________________ ride

c)  ____________________ run

d)  ____________________ leave

2 Fill in the blank with the best irregular **past tense** verb.

bought	flew	found	slept

a) The cat ____________________ all day yesterday.

b) The girl ____________________ to Ottawa last week.

c) My mom ____________________ her lost earring at breakfast.

d) I ____________________ a chocolate bar at the store this morning.

Adjectives

An **adjective** is a describing word.
A describing word tells a detail about a person, place, or thing.

*Examples: She has a **red** ball.* ⟶ The describing word is ***red***.
*The boy is **happy**.* ⟶ The describing word is ***happy***.

1. Fill in the blank with an **adjective** that describes the noun.

a) The ______________________________ cat chased the mouse.

b) My sister has a ______________________________ bike.

c) The ______________________________ tree swayed in the wind.

d) The ______________________________ flowers smelled sweet.

2. Circle the **adjective** in the sentence.

a) She wore a blue hat.

b) The fluffy cat slept.

c) The happy children played.

d) The big dog ran.

3. Write a sentence using **adjectives**.

____

Adjectives: Describing Nouns

An **adjective** is a word that is used to describe a person, place, or thing.

Use green to colour the boxes that contain **adjectives**.

pretty	dull	silly	cool
dog	yellow	T-shirt	apple
funny	boy	pink	cold
girl	blue	Winnipeg	sharp
beach	fast	warm	book

Adjective Dog Poem

1 Fill in the chart with **adjectives** that describe dogs.

Colour	Size
Shape	**Texture**
Number	**Sound**

Poem Checklist

- ☐ I used an adjective to describe colour.
- ☐ I used an adjective to describe size.
- ☐ I used an adjective to describe shape.
- ☐ I used an adjective to describe texture.
- ☐ I used an adjective to describe number.
- ☐ I used an adjective to describe sound.

Adjective Dog Poem (cont.)

2 Use your **adjectives** that describe dogs to fill in the poem. Decorate your poem.

Dogs!

Dogs, dogs, dogs,

________________ **dogs,**

________________ **dogs,**

________________, ________________, ________________, **dogs,**

________________ **dogs,**

These adjectives describe a dog!

________________ **dogs,**

________________ **dogs,**

And ________________ **dogs, too,**

________________, ________________, **dogs,**

Just to name a few!

I love ________________ **dogs!**

Adjectives: Describing Words

An **adjective** is a word that is used to describe a person, place, or thing.

Colour the pictures. Circle the **adjectives** that could be used to describe the person, place, or thing.

1  **Bananas** yummy yellow ugly curly sweet

2 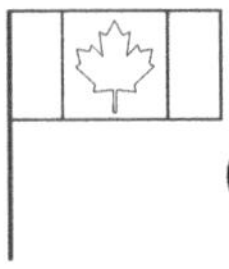 **Canada** beautiful funny large happy cold

3  **Teacher** smart blue shiny cheerful red

4  **My Friend** funny sour cool purple friendly

5  **Doctor** smart ask caring run nice

Articles: A and An

The words ***a*** and ***an*** are special adjectives called **articles.**

Use ***a*** before words that start with a consonant sound.

***a* flower**

Use ***an*** before words that start with a vowel sound.

***an* apple**

Print the correct **article** for the word.

1 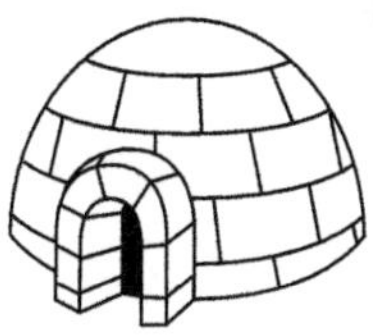
_____ igloo

2 
_____ mitten

3 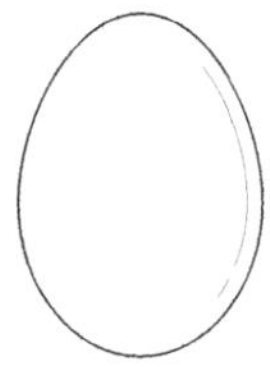
_____ egg

4 
_____ fish

5 
_____ owl

6 
_____ net

7 
_____ sock

8 
_____ bat

9 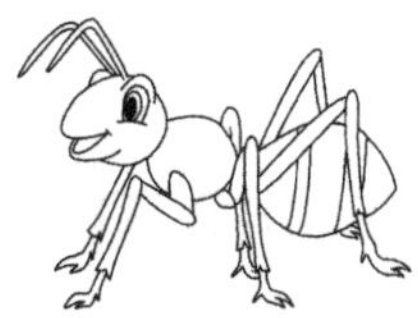
_____ ant

Colour the *a* words. red   Colour the *an* words. green

Prepositions: Place

A **preposition** is a word that tells you where something is or when something happened, such as **under** or **with**.

Example: The girl is ***under*** *the box.*

1 Fill in the blank with the **preposition** that fits best (**under** or **with**).

a) We sat ______________ an umbrella when it rained.

b) I ate my spaghetti ______________ a spoon and fork.

c) My teddy bear got left ______________ my bed.

d) I put my lunchbox ______________ my desk.

e) I like to eat French fries ______________ ketchup.

2 Write a sentence using the **preposition under** or **with**.

____

Prepositions: Time

A **preposition** is a word that tells you where something is or when something happened, such as **before** or **after**.

*Example: We went to the beach **after** school.*

1. Fill in the blank with the **preposition** that fits best (**before** or **after**).

a) I brush my teeth ____________ I go to bed.

b) I look both ways ____________ I cross the street.

c) I ate my dessert ____________ my dinner.

d) I put on my socks ____________ I put on my shoes.

e) I can watch TV ____________ I do my homework.

2. Write a sentence using the **preposition before** or **after**.

____

Conjunctions: *And*

A **conjunction** is a word that joins together two short sentences.

The word **and** is a conjunction.

Example: Jamal bought crayons. He drew pictures.

Jamal bought crayons, ***and*** *he drew pictures.*

Use the word **and** to join together the two ideas in the sentences.

1. I brought a sandwich for lunch. I ate it.

   ____

2. I like apples. I like bananas.

   ____

3. I bought a toy car. I bought a hockey stick.

   ____

4. I went to the waterpark. I went to the museum.

   ____

Conjunctions: *But*

A **conjunction** is a word that joins together two short sentences.

The word **but** is used to join two contrasting ideas together.

Example: Ling wants to stay up late. Her mom said no.

Ling wants to stay up late, ***but*** *her mom said no.*

Use the word **but** to join together the two ideas in the sentences.

1. I wanted a spoon for cereal. I only had a fork.

   ____

2. I painted a picture. I lost it.

   ____

3. I wanted to play outside. It was raining.

   ____

4. I wanted to play a game. The computer did not work.

   ____

Contractions

A **contraction** is a short word made by joining two words together. Use an apostrophe to replace one or more letters.

Examples: *You are* ☞ *You're*

I am ☞ *I'm*

1. Match the two words to their contraction.

I am	You're
You are	He's
She will	I'm
He is	They'll
You have	She'll
They will	You've

Contractions (cont.)

A **contraction** is a short word made by joining two words together.

Use an apostrophe to replace one or more letters.

Examples: Will not ☞ Won't *Do not ☞ Don't*

Cannot ☞ Can't *Was not ☞ Wasn't*

2 Match the two words to their contraction.

Is not ●	● Won't
Cannot ●	● Aren't
Do not ●	● Isn't
Will not ●	● Don't
Was not ●	● Can't
Are not ●	● Wasn't

Reading Strategies

Use these helpful tips when you get stuck on a word. Colour the pictures.

Eagle Eye

Look at the picture.

What is in the picture that starts with the beginning sound?

Lips the Fish

Get your mouth ready!

Say the beginning sound right away.

Chunky Monkey

Break the word into chunks and small words you know!

B ag   Fl ag

Re-Tryin' Lion

Re-read the sentence.

Think, "*What makes sense?*"

Reading Strategies (cont.)

Use these helpful tips when you get stuck on a word. Colour the pictures.

Stretchy Snake

Slowly stretch each letter sound to read the word.

s - t - r - e - t - c - h

Skippy Squirrel

Skip the tricky words. Read to the end.

Go back and try to re-read the words.

Flippy Dolphin

Flip the vowel sounds. If the short vowel sound does not work, try the long vowel sound.

Careful Chameleon

Carefully read the whole word. Think about the word parts.

Think, *"What makes sense?"*

Reading Comprehension

Help your child develop and reinforce essential reading comprehension skills.

Before Reading - Make Predictions

- What do you think the story/text will be about? Use pictures as clues.

While Reading - Check for Understanding

Author's Purpose

- Is the author trying to persuade, inform, or entertain the reader? How do you know?

Story Structure

- Is this text fact or fiction?
- What is this reading/story/text mostly about?
- Where does this story take place?
- Who is telling the story? How do you know?
- Who are the characters? How are they important to the story?
- What is the problem in the story?

After Reading - Responding to the Text

- If you could give this text another title, what would be?
- Retell the story in your own words.
- What happened in the beginning/middle/end of the story?
- Who is your favourite character?
- Did you like the ending of the story? Tell why.
- Which parts of the story could or could not happen in real life?

Making Connections

- How does the text remind you about what you already know?

Text-to-Self	Text-to-Text	Text-to-World
How does this text relate to your own life?	How is this text similar to or different from something you have read before?	What does this text remind you of in the real world?

Non-Fiction Text Features

Text features help the reader to understand the text better.
Here is a list of text features with a brief explanation on how they help the reader.

Table of Contents	Here the reader will find a list that provides the page numbers of the contents of the text.	Chapter 1....page 1 Chapter 2....page 5 Chapter 3....page 9
Heading	Here the reader will find a title of a section that lets the reader know what the section is about.	**Dogs** ← Dogs are a favourite pet to have.
Glossary	Here the reader will find a list of words that have definitions of what they mean.	Dogs Cats
Diagram and Illustration	A diagram will show the reader an image that shows the parts of something. An illustration shows a drawing of an object.	
Label	A label tells the reader the title of a map, a diagram, or an illustration. Labels also draw attention to the details of a picture.	
Caption	Captions are words that are placed underneath the illustrations. Captions give the reader more information about the map, diagram, or illustration.	
Map	Maps help the reader understand where something is happening. It is a visual representation of a location.	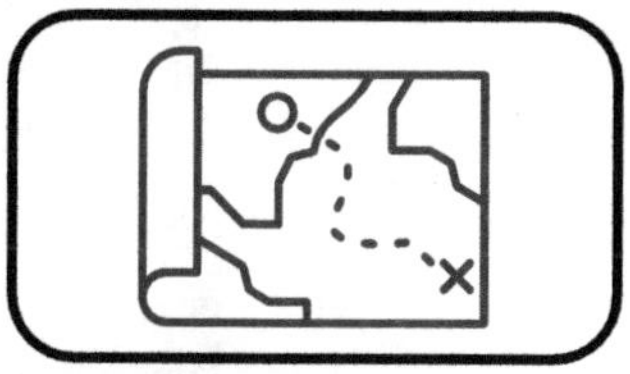
Fact Box	A fact box tells the reader extra information about the topic.	I have three dogs. Fact Box! Dogs are the most popular pet!

Unit 1

A Trip to the Zoo

A **text** is a piece of writing that you can read.
The **main idea** is what the text is mostly about.

Mom said, "Katie, I have a surprise for you. Today we will go to the zoo."

Katie clapped her hands and jumped up and down. "I want to see the monkeys first," she said. "I like to watch them play with each other. Then maybe we can go see the lions and tigers and elephants."

Mom looked out the window. "We might need our umbrellas. Katie, can you please put our umbrellas by the door so we don't forget them?"

Katie ran to get the umbrellas. "Mom," she called. "We don't have to see the snakes, do we?"

"No," answered Mom. "We can skip seeing the snakes if you like."

"Okay, good!" said Katie. "We are going to have a fun day!"

A Trip to the Zoo - Think About It!

Narrative text is a type of writing used to tell a story. It can be a real story about something that happened or it can be a made up story!

Circle the correct answer.

1. What is the main idea of the story?

    a) a trip to the zoo   b) a trip to the mall

2. What is the surprise that Mom has for Katie?

    a) They are going to the beach.
    b) They are going to the zoo.
    c) They are going to the park.
    d) They are going to the movies.

3. Which animal does Katie want to see first at the zoo?

    a) snakes   b) lions   c) monkeys

4. Why did Mom say they might need their umbrellas?

    a) To play with them   b) To keep them safe
    c) To watch them   d) To keep them dry

5. What must Mom have seen when she looked out the window?

    a) dark clouds   b) fog
    c) a sunny blue sky   d) snow

A Trip to the Zoo – Think About It! (cont.)

6 Draw a line to match who said what.

Katie's mom

Katie

- "We are going to have a fun day!"
- "Today we will go to the zoo."

7 Pick the correct word to fill in the blank.

a) Mom told Katie they were going to the ______________________.
(beach, park, zoo, mall)

b) Mom asked Katie to put their ______________________ by the door.
(shoes, toys, umbrellas, books)

c) Katie didn't want to see the ______________________ at the zoo.
(lions, snakes, butterflies, fish)

d) Katie was excited to have a ______________________ day at the zoo.
(boring, rainy, sunny, fun)

A Trip to the Zoo – Think About It! (cont.)

8 What animal would you like to see at a zoo? Tell why.

Draw a picture.

☐ I used capitals and end marks. ☐ My printing is neat. ☐ My writing makes sense.

A Day at the Beach

Marco and his parents sat on a big blanket at the beach. It was a sunny and windy day. The wind made big waves in the lake. There were lots of people at the beach. Everybody was talking and laughing.

Suddenly, a woman started shouting. Everybody on the beach got quiet so they could hear what she was saying.

"Spot, where are you?" the woman shouted. "Has anybody seen a small white and brown dog?" The woman walked down the beach calling, "Spot! Spot!"

Marco looked over at the lake. He saw a dog swimming to the shore. He wondered if the dog was Spot. When the dog came out of the water, Marco called, "Spot! Come here, Spot!"

The dog ran over to Marco and onto his family's blanket. "You must be Spot," said Marco. The dog wagged its tail and shook the water out of its fur. Marco and his parents got all wet!

Marco's dad waved at the woman and pointed to the dog. She rushed over. "You found my dog!" she said. "I didn't find your dog," said Dad. "My son did."

"I'm so thankful you found him," the woman said to Marco. She gave Marco a big hug. Just then, Spot saw a bird and ran off down the beach to chase it. The woman raced after Spot, shouting, "You naughty dog, Spot! Come back here!"

A Day at the Beach – Think About It!

1. What is the main idea of the story?

    a) Marco and his family had a boring day at the beach.
    b) Marco helped find a lost dog at the beach.
    c) The beach was very crowded and noisy.
    d) The woman never found her dog, Spot.

2. Fill in the blank using information from the story.

    a) Marco and his parents sat on a big ______________ at the beach.

    b) The wind made big ______________ in the lake.

    c) Everybody on the beach got ______________ when the woman started shouting.

    d) The woman rushed over to Marco and gave him a big ______________ to thank him for finding her dog.

    e) Spot saw a ______________ and ran off down the beach to chase it.

A Day at the Beach – Think About It! (cont.)

3. Number the events in order of what happened in the story.

_____ Marco saw a dog. The dog came to Marco.

_____ She rushed over, thanking Marco for finding her dog.

_____ A woman started shouting. She was looking for her dog Spot.

_____ Spot went onto the blanket. They all got wet.

_____ Marco and his parents went to the beach.

_____ Marco's dad waved at the woman.

4. Draw a line to match who said what.

Marco

"Has anybody seen a small white and brown dog?"

Dog Owner

"You must be Spot,"

A Day at the Beach – Think About It! (cont.)

5 Have you ever been to the beach on a sunny and windy day? What was it like?

Draw a picture.

☐ I used capitals and end marks. ☐ My printing is neat. ☐ My writing makes sense.

Unit 3

Plants Are All Around

Plants are all around us. Grass, flowers, bushes, and trees are all different kinds of plants.

Forests

Forests are full of trees. Some forest animals make their homes in trees. Birds build nests in trees. Some squirrels make homes in tree branches. Other squirrels live in holes they find inside trees.

Gardens

People grow plants in gardens at their homes. Many garden plants have flowers. One tulip plant grows only one flower. One rosebush can grow many roses.

Farms

Farmers grow plants that give us food. The corn, carrots, and potatoes people buy in stores all come from plants that farmers grew. Some farmers grow wheat, which we use to make bread.

Underwater

Did you know that some plants grow underwater? Seaweed grows in lakes and oceans. Seals and sea turtles eat seaweed. Some people eat seaweed, too! Seaweed is a healthy food because it has lots of vitamins.

Plants Are All Around – Think About It!

An **informational text** helps us learn about a topic by giving us facts and details.

1. What is the main idea of this text?

   a) Animals live in trees
   b) Gardens have many plants
   c) Plants are important to us
   d) Seaweed is good for us

2. Complete the sentence using information from the text.

   a) Birds build ________________________ in trees.

   b) A ________________________ plant grows only one flower.

   c) One rosebush can grow ________________________ roses.

   d) Farmers grow plants that give us ________________________.

   e) Seals and ____________________________ eat seaweed.

3. Which kind of plant do people use to make bread?

   a) wheat b) carrot
   c) seaweed d) tulip

Plants Are All Around – Think About It! (cont.)

A **heading** is a title of a section that lets the reader know what the section is about.

4. Under which heading in the text can you find information on seals and sea turtles?

   a) Forests b) Gardens c) Farms d) Underwater

5. Under which heading in the text can you find information about farmers?

   a) Forests b) Gardens c) Farms d) Underwater

6. Draw two foods you eat that come from plants.
   Write a label at the bottom to tell the name of each food.

Plants Are All Around – Think About It! (cont.)

7. Write four facts you learned about plants.

Forests

____

____

____

Gardens

____

____

____

Farms

____

____

____

Underwater

____

____

____

The Lost Keys

One sunny morning, Yolanda was getting ready for school. She was excited to go to school and see her friends. Just as Yolanda was going out, she couldn't find her keys. She had forgotten where she had put them.

Yolanda searched high and low in her room. She looked under her bed, and in her closet. She also checked her backpack. But the keys were lost. Yolanda was upset. She needed the keys to her bike lock to go to school. She didn't want to be late for school. She also did not want to miss her bike ride.

Yolanda's mom heard her crying and came to her room. She asked Yolanda what was wrong. Yolanda explained that she had lost her keys and didn't know where to find them.

Yolanda and her mom looked high and low for the keys. All of a sudden, Yolanda saw her keys. The keys were on the windowsill by the kitchen sink. Yolanda was so happy to find her keys! She gave her mom a big hug.

Yolanda's mom said it's okay to ask for help when she needed it. Yolanda learned she could rely on her mom for help with problems. Her mom would always be there to help her find a solution.

Yolanda felt relieved. She put her keys in her pocket, hopped on her bike, and rode to school. Yolanda got to school on time. She even had a few extra minutes to play with her friends!

The Lost Keys – Think About It

1. What was Yolanda looking for?

____

2. Why was Yolanda upset when she couldn't find her keys?

   a) She didn't want to ride her bike.
   b) She needed the keys to her bike lock to go to school.
   c) She didn't like school.

3. Yolanda found her keys on the __________ by the kitchen sink.

   a) windowsill   b) bed   c) closet

4. Yolanda felt __________ after finding her keys.

   a) excited   b) upset   c) relieved

5. What lesson did Yolanda learn from this experience?

   a) It's important to always find your keys.
   b) It's okay to ask for help when you have a problem.
   c) It's not okay to cry when you have a problem.

6. Use the expression "searched high and low" in a sentence.

____

The Lost Keys – Think About It (cont.)

7. Match the following characters with their role in the story:

Yolanda ●	● helped look for the lost keys
Yolanda's mom ●	● lost her keys before going to school

8. Draw a picture of Yolanda's room.
Label the different places she looked for her keys.

The Lost Keys – Think About It (cont.)

9 Create a lost poster.

Lost

For: ______________________

Please call:

Reward:

Who or what? ______________________

When last seen? ______________________

Where last seen? ______________________

Description: ______________________

____

____

☐ I used capitals and end marks. ☐ My printing is neat. ☐ My writing makes sense.

Unit 5 Occupations: X-ray Technician

Have you or has anyone in your family ever had an X-ray? If so, you probably know that an X-ray is a machine that sees inside a person's body. When someone has an illness or has a hurt arm or leg, an X-ray helps doctors understand what is going on and what they can do to help patients.

When a patient arrives to have an X-ray, an X-ray technician asks the patient questions about the problem. The technician explains what will happen and what the patient needs to do. The technician helps get the patient in the correct position for the X-ray.

After the patient has had an X-ray, a doctor looks at the X-ray and decides what to do next.

X-ray technicians also take care of the equipment they use. They usually work in hospitals, clinics, or doctor's offices.

A doctor looks at the X-ray

X-ray Technician – Think About It!

1. What is an X-ray used for?

   a) To see inside a person's body
   b) To help patients go to sleep
   c) To give patients medicine
   d) To play games

2. Why do doctors use X-rays?

   a) To help patients go to sleep
   b) To give patients medicine
   c) To see inside a person's body and understand what is going on
   d) To play games

3. Who helps patients get in the right position for an X-ray?

   a) The nurse
   b) The X-ray technician
   c) The patient

4. What happens after a patient has had an X-ray?

   a) The patient goes home
   b) The technician looks at the X-ray
   c) The doctor looks at the X-ray and decides what to do next
   d) The technician cleans the X-ray machine

X-ray Technician – Think About It! (cont.)

5. Fill in the blank using information from the reading.

An X-ray helps doctors ________ what they can do to help patients.

a) avoid b) understand c) ignore d) overlook

6. Fill in the blank using information from the reading.

X-ray technicians do not work in ____________________________.

a) clinics b) doctor's offices c) hospitals d) parks

7. Match the following vocabulary words to their meanings:

X-ray machine	A machine that sees inside a person's body
X-ray technician	Tools or instruments used for a particular purpose.
Illness	A person who operates an X-ray machine.
Equipment	A problem or sickness in the body.

X-ray Technician – Think About It! (cont.)

8. Pretend you are a doctor looking at an X-ray. Can you describe what you see? Is there anything that looks different or unusual?

____

____

____

____

____

____

Draw a picture.

☐ I used capitals and end marks. ☐ My printing is neat. ☐ My writing makes sense.

Unit 6

Occupations: Air Traffic Controller

Have you ever wondered how pilots know how to keep a plane a safe distance away from other airplanes in the sky? After all, there are no traffic lights in the air.

Every airport has air traffic controllers to do just that. Air traffic controllers use computers to carefully watch where and how planes are coming and going. They tell pilots if there is another plane near them. They also help organize how planes take off and land from airports. Most of the air traffic controllers sit in a special tower.

You have to be alert and organized if you are an air traffic controller. You need to be good at math. You have to spend many hours training for the job. Sometimes you have to work nights or on weekends.

An air traffic controller is an exciting job. It's also a very important job. It keeps people safe.

Air traffic controllers

Air Traffic Controller – Think About It!

1. Match the vocabulary word to its meaning.

Air traffic controller ●		● A tall structure where air traffic controllers sit to watch and manage planes.
Flight path ●		● Someone who helps organize how planes take off and land from airports
Airport tower ●		● The route that a plane takes when flying from one place to another

2. What is the job of an air traffic controller?

   a) Someone who flies planes.

   b) Someone who sells plane tickets.

   c) Someone who helps organize how planes take off and land at airports.

3. If an air traffic controller saw two planes getting too close to each other, what should they do?

   a) Nothing

   b) Tell the pilots to change their flight path

   c) Call the airport manager

Air Traffic Controller – Think About It! (cont.)

4. Air traffic controllers use computers to carefully watch where and how planes are coming and going.

   a) True   b) False

5. Air traffic controllers do not help organize how planes take off and land from airports.

   a) True   b) False

6. An air traffic controller does not need to be good at math.

   a) True   b) False

7. An air traffic controller job is not very important.

   a) True   b) False

8. Air traffic controllers sit in a special tower at the airport to monitor and control air traffic.

   a) True   b) False

9. What is the purpose of this text?

   a) inform   b) persuade   c) entertain

Air Traffic Controller – Think About It! (cont.)

10 Air traffic controllers are important for keeping people safe in the skies.

Draw a picture.

Let me tell you why.

First of all, ____

____

Another reason is ____

____

Finally, ____

____

____

☐ I used capitals and end marks. ☐ My printing is neat. ☐ My writing makes sense.

Unit 7 Aisha Goes to a New School

When Aisha started her new school, she didn't know anyone. Aisha felt excited and nervous. She was from Syria and spoke little English.

When Aisha came into the classroom, she saw many children. They were friendly and said hello to her in different languages. Some said "Hola," which is Spanish. Some said "Bonjour," which is French.

The teacher asked the class to make Aisha feel welcome. Everyone wanted to help. Maya said, "My family is from China, and we say 'Ni hào' to say hello." Then Andrew said, "My family is from Greece, and we say 'Yassou.'"

At snack time, Aisha shared some hummus and chips. It was yummy. All the kids wanted to try it! All day long, Aisha made new friends. They showed her around the school and helped her with her English.

At the end of the day, Aisha said goodbye to her new friends. She thanked them for being so kind to her. She was excited to come back to school the next day to learn more. The kids waved goodbye. They called out, "Adios," which means goodbye in Spanish.

Aisha Goes to a New School – Think About It!

1. Match the word to its meaning.

"Hola"		Hello in Greek
"Bonjour"		Hello in Chinese
"Ni hao"		Hello in Spanish
"Yassou"		Hello in French

2. Fill in the blank using the information from the story.

a) On Aisha's first day at her new school, she didn't know

______________________________.
(anyone, anything, anywhere)

b) Aisha was from ________________________ and spoke little English.
(Syria, Spain, Italy)

c) At snack time, Aisha shared hummus and ________________________.
(pizza, chips, sushi)

d) The kids called out "Adios," which means goodbye in

________________________.
(Spanish, French, Arabic)

Aisha Goes to a New School – Think About It! (cont.)

3. Create a poster that welcomes new students to your school.
   Make sure:

   ☐ The poster has a welcoming message or greeting to new students.
   ☐ The poster is neat and has colourful pictures.

☐ I used capitals and end marks. ☐ My printing is neat. ☐ My writing makes sense.

Aisha Goes to a New School – Think About It! (cont.)

4 Write a letter to Aisha, welcoming her to your school.

____
DATE

Dear ________________________,
GREETING

BODY

____

____

____

____

____

____

____

____

Sincerely,

____
CLOSING / SIGNATURE

☐ I used capitals and end marks. ☐ My printing is neat. ☐ My writing makes sense.

Unit 8 Meet Max: My Furry and Friendly Dog

Descriptive writing uses words to create a picture in your mind. It helps us imagine how things look, feel, sound, and even smell!

Meet Max, my furry and friendly pet dog. He's a golden retriever with soft, fluffy fur. His fur is the colour of sunshine. Max has a big, wet nose. He has kind, brown eyes that sparkle when he sees me.

He loves to wag his tail back and forth. You see his big, shiny teeth when he is happy. Max's ears are floppy and hang down on the sides of his head. He has four furry paws that make a "click-click" sound on the floor when he walks.

Max is a handsome dog! Everyone who sees him says he's very cute. But to me, he's more than just cute. He is my best friend. I love him very much!

Meet Max: My Furry and Friendly Dog – Think About It!

1 Fill in the blank with an adjective from the word box:

cute	floppy	fluffy	furry	golden
handsome	kind	shiny	wag	wet

a) Meet Max, my ________________ and friendly pet dog.

b) Max is a ________________ retriever.

c) Max has soft, ________________ fur.

d) Max has a big, ________________ nose.

e) Max has ________________, brown eyes that sparkle.

f) Max has big, ________________ teeth.

g) Max's ears are ________________ and hang down.

h) He loves to ________________ his tail back and forth.

i) Max is a ________________ dog!

j) Everyone who sees him says he's very ________________.

Meet Max: My Furry and Friendly Dog – Think About It! (cont.)

2. Write a description of a pet. Include many details.

____

____

____

____

____

____

Draw a picture of the pet.

☐ I used capitals and end marks. ☐ My printing is neat. ☐ My writing makes sense.

A **diamante poem** is in the shape of a diamond.

3. Write a diamante poem about a pet.
The shape tells what types of words to use.

____
(noun)

________________ ________________
(adjective) (adjective)

________________ ________________ ________________
("ing" verb) ("ing" verb) ("ing" verb)

________________ ________________
(adjective) (adjective)

____
(noun)

Unit 9 How Do You Like Them Apples?

Apples are delicious! They come in many different colours such as red, green, and yellow. Apples are a type of fruit that grows on trees.

Did you know that there are many kinds of apples? Some apples are sweet and some are sour. I like sweet apples the best, but some people might like sour apples best. Apples are also good for you! They have vitamins and minerals that help keep your body healthy.

I think everyone should eat apples every day, but some people might not like them as much as I do. That's okay because everyone has different tastes!

How Do You Like Them Apples? – Think About It!

1 Write "Fact" if the sentence is true and can be proven.
Write "Opinion" if the sentence is a personal belief or feeling.

a) ________________ Everyone should eat apples every day.

b) ________________ Apples are a type of fruit that grow on trees.

c) ________________ There are many different colours of apples.

d) ________________ Some apples are sweet and some are sour.

e) ________________ Apples have vitamins and minerals.

2 Complete the word search. Circle the words as you find them.

A	P	P	L	E	L	Y	P
R	O	U	N	D	K	L	J
T	R	E	E	A	O	I	U
U	H	N	A	T	U	R	E
V	I	T	A	M	I	N	S
S	W	E	E	T	Q	W	E
H	G	E	D	S	O	U	R

Words to search for:

apple
nature
round
sour
sweet
tree
vitamins

How Do You Like Them Apples? – Think About It! (cont.)

3. Which colours can apples be?

    a) Green and blue
    b) Red, green, and yellow
    c) Black and white
    d) Orange and purple

4. What makes apples good for your body?

    a) They are sweet and tasty
    b) They have lots of sugar
    c) They have vitamins and minerals
    d) They are fun to eat

5. Why might someone prefer sour apples over sweet apples?

    a) Sour apples are healthier
    b) Sweet apples are too sugary
    c) Sour apples taste better to them
    d) Sweet apples are too expensive

6. List one way apples can be the same.

____

7. List one way apples can be different.

____

How Do You Like Them Apples? – Think About It! (cont.)

A **proverb** is a wise saying that offers some advice.

8. Draw the proverb below.

"**An apple a day keeps the doctor away.**"

9. Explain what you think the proverb means.

10. Do you think this is good advice? Explain your thinking.

☐ I used capitals and end marks. ☐ My printing is neat. ☐ My writing makes sense.

Unit 10

Thumper Makes a Friend

Thumper was a kind and friendly rabbit. He loved to hop and play around in the forest.

One day, Thumper tripped over a little bird who had fallen out of its nest. The bird was chirping and cheeping. He looked sad and scared.

Thumper knew just what to do. He hopped over to the bird and said, "Don't worry. I'll help you get back to your nest." The little bird said, "Thank you for helping me. You are very kind."

Thumper used his strong back legs to hop up to the bird's nest. He put the little bird safely back inside. The mother bird was very grateful to Thumper. She sang a beautiful song to thank him.

From that day on, Thumper and the bird became the best of friends. They played together every day. Thumper also helped the little bird find worms to eat.

Thumper felt happy knowing he helped someone in need.

Thumper Makes a Friend – Think About It!

1. Put the events in the order that they happened in the story.

    ______ Thumper helps the little bird get back to its nest.

    ______ Thumper finds the little bird who has fallen out of its nest.

    ______ Thumper and the little bird become the best of friends.

2. What is the name of the little rabbit in the story?

    a) Tigger   b) Thumper   c) Bugs Bunny

3. How did Thumper help the bird get back to its nest?

    a) He used a ladder
    b) He hopped up to the nest and placed the bird back inside
    c) He called for help

4. How did Thumper feel after he helped the little bird?

    a) angry   b) tired   c) happy   d) sad

A **caption** tells what a picture is about.

5. Write a caption below for the picture in the text.

____

Thumper Makes a Friend – Think About It! (cont.)

6 Complete the story map using information from the story.

Title

Setting

Characters

Problem

Solution

Thumper Makes a Friend – Think About It! (cont.)

7. Thumper was a good friend to the little bird.

Draw a picture.

I (agree   disagree) with this statement. Let me tell you why.

First of all, ____

____

Another reason is ____

____

Finally, ____

____

____

☐ I used capitals and end marks. ☐ My printing is neat. ☐ My writing makes sense.

Unit 11 Save Water to Help Your Planet!

Did you know that wasting water can hurt Earth? Using too much water can make it harder for plants and animals to get the water they need. So, everyone should save water to help Earth.

Try some of these ways to save water.

Turn Off the Tap:
When brushing your teeth, turn off the tap. This will save water. Also, turn off the tap when washing your hands or face.

Take Short Showers:
Take a quick shower instead of a bath. It saves water and energy!

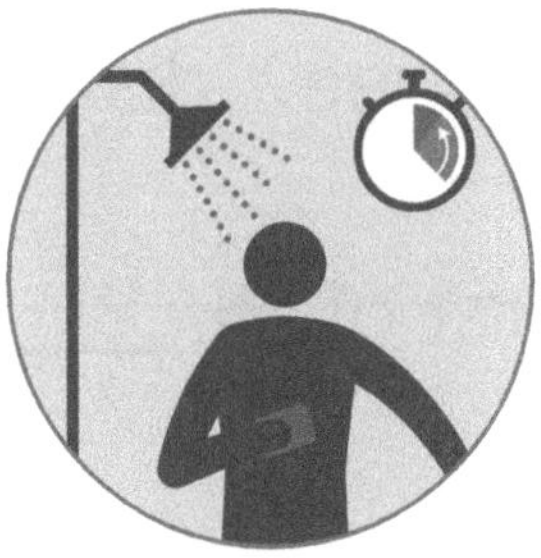

Water Your Plants Wisely:
Water your plants in the early morning or late afternoon. It's cooler and less windy, so less water will be lost.

Use a Bucket:
Use a bucket to wash your car, your bike, or your pet instead of a hose. It saves water!

Save Water to Help Your Planet! – Think About It!

This text tells about a **problem** that needs to be fixed.
This text also shows ways to **fix** the problem.
These are called **solutions**.

1. Choose the best word to fill in the blank.

problem	solution

a) Saving water is a ________________ for Earth.

b) Using too much water is a ________________ for Earth.

2. Fill in the blank.

bucket	healthy	shower	tap

a) When brushing your teeth, remember to turn off the ________________ to save water.

b) Taking a quick ________________ instead of a bath can save water and energy.

c) You can use a ________________ to wash your car, your bike, or your pet instead of a hose to save water.

d) Saving water is important because it helps keep plants and animals ________________.

3 How to Save Water: Tips for Kids!

Do	Don't
Do	**Don't**

Save Water to Help Your Planet! – Think About It! (cont.)

4. Create a poster to encourage people to save water. Use information from the text and your own ideas.

☐ I used capitals and end marks. ☐ My printing is neat. ☐ My writing makes sense.

Unit 12

Fun After School: A Day in the Life of Jack

Hi there! My name is Jack. This is what I did after school today. I always love this time because I get to do fun things with my family and friends.

First, I went to the park with my mom. We had a blast playing on the swings and going down the slide. It was fun to play catch, too!

Next, after playing, we walked back home. The weather was sunny. We enjoyed spending time together.

Then, we decided to bake some oatmeal cookies. I helped my mom mix the ingredients. I even got to lick the spoon! The oatmeal cookies turned out super delicious! I felt so proud of myself for helping to make them.

Finally, I still had time before dinner to play outside with my friends.

I love having lots of fun things to do after school.

A Day in the Life of Jack – Think About It!

A **recount text pattern** is a type of writing that tells about something that happened, often in the order it happened, with details and sometimes personal thoughts or feelings.

Read the passage about Jack's after-school adventures and answer the following questions:

1. What is the purpose of this text?

   a) To tell a story about something that happened
   b) To persuade the reader

2. Who is telling the story?

   a) Jack's mom   b) Jack

3. How was the weather during Jack's walk home from the park?

   a) cloudy   b) rainy   c) sunny

4. What did Jack help his mom do in the kitchen?

   a) Clean the kitchen
   b) Mix the ingredients for oatmeal cookies
   c) Wash the dishes

5. What is your favourite thing to do after school?

A Day in the Life of Jack – Think About It! (cont.)

6 Complete the graphic organizer to list the events in the story.

First...

Next...

Then...

Finally...

A Day in the Life of Jack – Think About It! (cont.)

7. Describe your best day ever.

My best day ever was when...

____

First, ____

Then, ____

Last, ____

That day made me feel... ______________________________

____

☐ I used capitals and end marks. ☐ My printing is neat. ☐ My writing makes sense.

Unit 13

Billy's Flat Tire

Billy loves going for bike rides after school. He likes the feeling of the wind on his face.

While riding his bike, Billy heard a loud hissing noise. He stopped his bike and looked down. The tire was flat. Billy felt sad because he knew he couldn't ride his bike. He had to fix the tire.

Billy pushed his bike back home. He went straight to his dad for help. His dad showed him how to take off the tire, then fix the flat and put the tire back on. Finally, Billy learned how to use a pump to blow up the tire. Billy watched closely. He learned how to fix a tire step by step.

After his dad had fixed the tire, Billy was happy again. He jumped on his bike and rode down the street. He felt the wind on his face and the sun on his back. He knew he could always count on his dad to help him. Billy also knew he could now fix a flat tire, too!

Billy's Flat Tire – Think About It!

1. Put the following events in the correct order.

_________ Billy went to his dad for help.

_________ Billy's dad helped him fix the tire.

_________ Billy pushed his bike back home.

_________ Billy's tire was flat.

A **cause** is what makes something happen.
The **effect** is what happens because of the cause.

2. Match the cause and effect using information from the story.

Cause	Effect
Billy heard a loud hissing noise while riding his bike ●	● Billy learned how to use a pump to blow up the tire.
Billy went to his dad for help ●	● Billy's tire was flat.
Billy watched closely as his dad fixed the tire ●	● Billy learned how to fix a tire step by step

Billy's Flat Tire – Think About It! (cont.)

3. Fill in the blank with the correct word.

fix	flat	hissing	pump	ride

a) I want to ____________ the Ferris wheel at the fair.

b) The ____________ of the balloon scared the cat.

c) The soccer ball was ____________, so we had to stop playing.

d) We need to use the ____________ to inflate the air mattress.

e) My mom can ____________ my broken necklace with some glue.

4. What does the story remind you of?

____

____

____

____

Billy's Flat Tire – Think About It! (cont.)

5. Pretend you are starting your own bike repair shop. Create an advertisement poster for your shop.

- Think of a fun name for your bike repair shop, like "Bike Fixers."
- List the services you offer, like fixing flat tires or putting chains on.
- Draw pictures for your bike repair shop ad.
- Make sure your message is clear and easy to read.

Unit 14

How to Make a Cake

Get ready to bake a yummy cake that will make your taste buds dance!

Step 1: Mix the cake batter.

Mix the cake mix with some water, oil, and eggs in a bowl. Keep mixing until there are no lumps.

Step 2: Bake the cake

Preheat the oven and put the cake batter in a greased cake pan. Bake it in the oven for the time on the box. Don't open the oven door too often.

Step 3: Decorate the cake

After the cake cools down, you can decorate it. Put frosting, sprinkles, or other toppings on it. Make it look special!

Step 4: Enjoy the cake

Now it's time to eat the cake! Cut a slice and taste the yummy flavours. Share with your family and friends to make them happy, too.

How to Make a Cake – Think About It!

1. Finish the sentence.

   Get ready to bake a ________________ cake that will make your

   ____.

2. Fill in the blank with the correct word.

eggs	frosting	greased	happy
oil	sprinkles	water	yummy

a) Mix the cake mix with __________, __________, and __________.

b) Put the cake batter in a __________________ cake pan.

c) Decorate the cake with __________, __________, or other toppings.

d) Cut a slice and taste the ____________ flavours.

e) Share with your family and friends to make them ____________.

How to Make a Cake – Think About It! (cont.)

A **procedure** is a set of steps to follow to make or do something. Examples of some procedures are recipes and instructions.

3 Use the pictures to write the steps telling how make a cake.

Step 1

Step 2

Step 3

Step 4

First, ______________________________

Next, ______________________________

Then, ______________________________

Last, ______________________________

☐ I used capitals and end marks. ☐ My printing is neat. ☐ My writing makes sense.

How to Make a Cake – Think About It! (cont.)

4 You've just baked a special cake! Create a post about your cake.

☐ I used capitals and end marks. ☐ My printing is neat. ☐ My writing makes sense.

Unit 15 Delicious Bannock

Bannock is bread made by Canada's First Nations people. They taught Canada's explorers and fur traders how to make it, too.

What Is in Bannock?

First Nations people have made bannock for hundreds of years. Long ago, they baked it using cornmeal and ground plant bulbs.

Bannock

Today, bannock is made using flour, baking powder, oil, and water. Sometimes people add spices. They may add dried fruit and flavouring, too.

Baking Bannock

Some First Nations people baked their bannock in clay or rock ovens. Others wrapped the dough around a stick and toasted it.

Bannock over fire

Some First Nations groups rolled their bannock in sand. Then they baked it in a fire pit. When it was done, they brushed off the sand. Then they ate the bannock.

Today, bannock is usually fried in a frying pan or baked in an oven. It is served at powwows, rodeos, and festivals.

Delicious Bannock – Think About It!

1. What is bannock?

    a) A type of cake
    b) A type of bread made by Canada's First Nations people
    c) A type of candy

2. List three ways First Nations people baked their bannock long ago.

3. Who did the First Nations people teach how to make bannock?

4. List 6 ingredients that First Nations people put in bannock today.

Delicious Bannock – Think About It! (cont.)

5. List three places where Bannock might be served.

____________ ____________ ____________

6. Match the ingredients used to make bannock with the correct time period.

Ingredients	Time Period
Cornmeal and ground plant bulbs ●	● Today
Flour, baking powder, oil and water ●	● Long ago

7. Count the syllables of each word. Sort them into the chart.

bannock **clay** **explorer** **festival**
nation **oil** **rodeo** **spices** **stick**

1 syllable	2 syllables	3 syllables
________	________	________
________	________	________
________	________	________

Delicious Bannock – Think About It! (cont.)

8. What is a traditional food that is special to your family?

Draw a picture.

A traditional food special to my family is ______________________________.

Let me tell you why.

____

____

____

____

☐ I used capitals and end marks. ☐ My printing is neat. ☐ My writing makes sense.

Unit 16 Dinosaur Park

Are you ready to take a trip back in time? Come to the Dinosaur Park in Alberta and explore the world of dinosaurs!

What Is Dinosaur Park?

Dinosaur Park is a special place to see real dinosaur bones. You also learn about the time when dinosaurs lived. It's like a big museum, but outside in nature!

What Can You Do There?

At the Dinosaur Park, you can:

Fossils

1. See real dinosaur bones and fossils up close.
2. Walk on trails and see the same rocks and hills the dinosaurs lived on.
3. Climb to the top of a lookout tower. Look at the view of the park from up high!
4. Have a picnic and enjoy being outside in nature.
5. Play in the playground and have fun.

Picnic area

Dinosaur Park is a great place for kids and adults who love dinosaurs and nature. It's an adventure you don't want to miss!

Dinosaur Park – Think About It!

Persuasive writing is when you try to convince someone to agree with your ideas or to do something you want them to do. You do this by giving good reasons and examples in your writing.

1 What is the main purpose of the text?

a) To inform readers about Dinosaur Park
b) To persuade readers to visit Dinosaur Park

2 How does the author try to persuade the readers?

a) By explaining the different activities at Dinosaur Park

b) By telling about the real dinosaur bones and fossils at the park

c) By saying that the park is great for kids and adults who love dinosaurs and nature

d) All of the above

3 Complete the word search. Circle the words as you find them.

P	A	L	B	E	R	T	A
D	I	N	O	S	A	U	R
Q	M	A	N	T	R	W	O
P	K	T	E	L	E	O	C
A	M	U	S	E	U	M	K
R	Q	R	U	W	V	J	S
K	Y	E	T	R	A	I	L

Words to search for:

Alberta	bones
dinosaur	museum
nature	park
rocks	trail

Dinosaur Park – Think About It! (cont.)

4. What is Dinosaur Park compared to in the text?

   a) A big museum inside a building

   b) A big museum outside in nature

   c) A small playground

5. You can see real dinosaur bones at Dinosaur Park.

   a) True b) False

6. At Dinosaur Park, you can only walk on the trails and can't see any rocks or hills.

   a) True b) False

7. You can climb to the top of a lookout tower at Dinosaur Park.

   a) True b) False

8. There is no picnic area at Dinosaur Park.

   a) True b) False

9. Only kids can visit Dinosaur Park.

   a) True b) False

Dinosaur Park – Think About It! (cont.)

10 If I visited Dinosaur Park for a day, I would do these things.

First, ______________________________

Next, ______________________________

Then, ______________________________

Finally, ______________________________

I feel ______________________________ to go!

☐ I used capitals and end marks. ☐ My printing is neat. ☐ My writing makes sense.

Unit 17

Similies

Have you ever heard of similes? They are sentences that compare two things using the words "like" or "as." Similes can make a story or description more interesting and fun to read! Just think of two things that are different but have something in common, and use "like" or "as" to compare them.

Here are some examples of similes:

The sun is as bright as a flashlight.

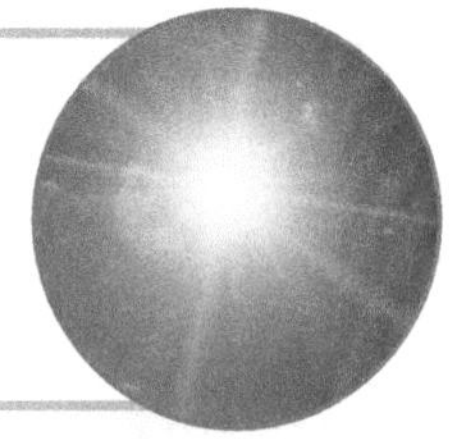

The water sparkles like diamonds in the sunshine.

My dog is as fast as a cheetah when he chases his toy.

The clouds are like fluffy cotton candy in the sky.

Next time you write a story or describe something, try using similes to make it more interesting!

Similies – Think About It!

1. What are similes?

   a) Sentences that describe things
   b) Sentences that compare two things using "like" or "as"
   c) Sentences that ask questions

2. Find and underline the simile in the sentence.

   a) The cat's fur is as soft as a blanket.

   b) The popcorn popped like fireworks in the microwave.

   c) The snow is as white as a polar bear's fur.

   d) My cousin is as smart as a fox.

   e) The tree branches are like arms reaching up to the sky.

3. Pick a simile from above. Draw a picture.

Similies – Think About It! (cont.)

4. Finish the sentence by creating a simile using "like" or "as."

a) The moon is as ____________________________________.

b) The ocean waves are like ____________________________.

c) My friend's smile is as ______________________________.

d) The stars twinkle like ______________________________.

5. Match the simile on the left with its meaning on the right.

As quiet as a mouse ●	● Very cunning or sneaky
As brave as a lion ●	● Very busy or active
As busy as a bee ●	● Very brave
As sly as a fox ●	● Very quiet

Similies – Think About It! (cont.)

6. A **simile poem** contains similes to compare and describe an object or action. Similes use "like" or "as" to compare.

For example:

The sun is like a golden ball,
High up in the sky so tall,
It shines so bright for all to see,
Like a giant lamp, it lights up our day with glee.

Write your own simile poem. Decorate your poem.

Unit 18 Earth Day

Earth Day is April 22 every year. It is a day to think about our planet. On Earth Day, people help keep Earth clean and safe.

Earth Day Around the World

People all over the world take part in Earth Day. More than one billion people help out. Earth Day lets people know what they can do to help keep Earth clean.

Earth Day reminds people to take care of the planet. We can cut down on pollution. We can use water carefully.

How You Can Help

Do not wait until Earth Day to help the planet. There are many ways you can help. You can pick up litter. You can recycle paper and cardboard. You help the planet when you reduce how much garbage you throw out.

Planting a garden helps, too. On Earth Day, some groups plant trees.

Earth Day is an important day. Find out how you can help in your area.

Fact Box!

About 1 billion people recognize Earth Day each year.

Earth Day – Think About It!

1. Why did the author write this text?

    a) To show how to make the planet dirty
    b) To describe Earth Day and how to help the planet
    c) To ignore the planet

2. When is Earth Day?

    a) April 22   b) May 22   c) March 22

3. How can you help the planet on Earth Day?

    a) By making more garbage
    b) By picking up litter
    c) By ignoring the planet

4. Why is Earth Day an important day?

    a) Because it is a day to make the planet dirty
    b) Because it is a day to ignore the planet
    c) Because it is a day to remind people to take care of the planet

5. What is another word for litter?

    a) trash   b) treasure   c) toys   d) trees

6. What do you learn from the fact box in the text?

____

Earth Day – Think About It! (cont.)

7 Complete the Earth Day Poster.

LOVE YOUR PLANET

I can reduce:

Earth Day – Think About It! (cont.)

An **acrostic poem** is a special type of poem where you use the first letter of each word to spell out a message or a word.

8 Write an acrostic poem about Earth Day. Decorate your poem with pictures or colours that remind you of Earth Day.

E ______________________________

A ______________________________

R ______________________________

T ______________________________

H ______________________________

Unit 19 Dinosaurs Big and Small

Compare and contrast text is a type of writing that tells you how two things are alike (compare) and how they are different (contrast).

T-Rex

The first T-Rex bones were discovered more than 100 years ago. T-Rex was a big dinosaur, but it was not the biggest. A T-Rex was longer than a large school bus. This dinosaur hunted for its food. It had many strong teeth to help it catch and eat animals. A T-Rex did not use its arms to bring food to its mouth. Its arms were too short to reach its mouth.

Some scientists believe that young T-Rex dinosaurs had feathers covering their body. But a T-Rex did not have wings, so it could not fly. As a T-Rex got older, the feathers fell off.

Dilong

The first Dilong bones were discovered in 2004. Dilong (say it like this: die-long) was one of the smaller dinosaurs. It was only about as long as a bed for a grownup. Like a T-Rex, a Dilong hunted animals for food and used its many strong teeth to eat them. A Dilong could use its arms to help it eat. This dinosaur's arms were long enough to reach up to its mouth. Scientists believe that Dilongs had feathers. The feathers did not fall out as the dinosaurs got older. A Dilong did not have wings, so it could not fly.

Dinosaurs Big and Small – Think About It!

1 What two dinosaurs are compared in this text?

____

2 How do you think having feathers helped a Dilong?

a) Feathers helped a Dilong fly.
b) Feathers helped a Dilong stay warm.
c) Feathers helped a Dilong hunt for food.
d) Feathers helped a Dilong run faster.

3 What does the word "discovered" mean in the sentence "The first T-Rex bones were discovered more than 100 years ago"?

a) found
b) lost
c) made

A **cause** is what makes something happen.
The **effect** is what happens because of the cause.

4 Write **Cause** or **Effect** beside each sentence.

____________________: Scientists can tell how big a dinosaur was.

____________________: Scientists look at a dinosaur's bones.

Dinosaurs Big and Small – Think About It! (cont.)

5. Write each piece of information in the correct box.

- many strong teeth
- had feathers when older
- arms helped it eat
- hunted animals for food

T-Rex and Dilong	Only Dilong
____________________	____________________
____________________	____________________

6. Write "True" or "False" on the line next to each statement.

a) ______________ A T-Rex was longer than a large school bus.

b) ______________ A T-Rex used its arms to bring food to its mouth.

c) ______________ As a T-Rex got older, the feathers fell off.

d) ______________ Dilongs had feathers that fell off as they got older.

e) ______________ Dilongs could fly with their wings.

f) ______________ A Dilong was about as long as a bed for a grownup.

g) ______________ T-Rex was the biggest dinosaur.

Dinosaurs Big and Small – Think About It! (cont.)

7. It would be scary to encounter a (T-Rex Dilong) in real life.

First of all, ____

____

Another reason is, ____

____

Finally, ____

____

Draw a picture.

☐ I used capitals and end marks. ☐ My printing is neat. ☐ My writing makes sense.

Occupations: Baker

Kneading dough

Do you like fresh bread? Do you like cakes, doughnuts, cupcakes, and cookies? Bakers make all those delicious foods. They mix ingredients, prepare equipment, measure, weigh, and knead dough, roll it out, and shape it. They follow recipes so their breads, cookies, and cakes come out just right and just the same every time.

Some bakers work at big companies, making large amounts of baked goods. They work with big mixing machines and ovens.

Fresh bread

Other bakers work in smaller bakeries. Sometimes they own their own bakery. Sometimes they specialize in a certain kind of baked goods like cupcakes or doughnuts. Many bakers have to work in the middle of the night so there's fresh bread for their customers in the morning.

Cake decorating

To become a baker, you often take a special course. You study nutrition, handling food safely, baking, and cake decorating. Some people train with experienced bakers right on the job.

Occupations: Baker – Think About It!

1. What does “knead” mean in the sentence “They knead dough, roll it out, and shape it”?

   a) to cut
   b) to mix
   c) to shape
   d) to press and fold

2. What does “specialize” mean in the sentence “Sometimes they specialize in a certain kind of baked goods”?

   a) to work for a big company
   b) to own a bakery
   c) to focus on one kind of baked good
   d) to work at night

3. Fill in the blank with the correct word.

bakery	cupcakes	doughnuts	recipe

a) A ________________ is a list of ingredients for making a dish.

b) A baker can specialize in ________________ or ________________.

c) A ________________ is where baked goods are made and sold.

Occupations: Baker – Think About It! (cont.)

4 Match the equipment with its use.

	mixing machine ●	● weigh ingredients
	oven ●	● mix ingredients together
	scale ●	● bake the dough
	rolling pin ●	● flatten and shape the dough

5 Write **Fact** or **Opinion** on the line next to the statement.

a) ______________ To become a baker, you often take a special course.

b) ______________ Cupcakes are the best kind of baked good.

6 What is your favourite baked good?

____

____

Occupations: Baker – Think About It! (cont.)

7 You have just baked a cupcake. Draw toppings on your cupcake.

How does it look?

How does it smell?

How does it taste?

How does it feel?

☐ I used capitals and end marks. ☐ My printing is neat. ☐ My writing makes sense.

Wayne Gretzky

A **biography** is a text that tells true and interesting facts about a person's life.

When Wayne Gretzky was only 10 years old, he scored 378 goals. That was in just 68 games! Even then, people called him "the Great One."

Out on the Backyard Rink

Wayne was born in 1961 in Brantford, Ontario. Like many Canadian kids, he began playing hockey on a rink in his backyard. Wayne skated and shot pucks for hours. He loved hockey so much that it never felt like practicing to him.

Wayne joined the National Hockey League (NHL) in 1979. Just like when he was a kid, he often tired his teammates with long practices.

Record Setter

Wayne wasn't big and his style wasn't smooth. But he had an incredibly accurate shot and an amazing instinct for playing hockey.

Wayne retired from playing hockey in 1999. By that time, he had set or tied 61 NHL records. He's still the League's all-time leading scorer, with 2857 points. Wayne is the only player to reach 2000 career points.

Fact Box!

Wayne's jersey #99 was retired by all the teams in the NHL.

Wayne Gretzky – Think About It!

1. What is the main idea of the text?

   a) Wayne Gretzky was a great hockey player.

   b) Hockey is a popular sport in Canada.

   c) Wayne Gretzky had a difficult childhood.

   d) Wayne Gretzky didn't like practicing hockey.

2. Why did the author write this text?

   a) To teach readers about the sport of hockey

   b) To entertain readers with a story about a famous athlete

   c) To persuade readers to become hockey players

   d) To inform readers about the life and accomplishments of Wayne Gretzky

3. What was Wayne Gretzky called when he was only 10 years old?

   a) "The Good One" b) "The Great One"

   c) "The Cool One" d) "The Big One"

4. How many goals did Wayne score when he was only 10 years old?

   a) 78 goals b) 278 goals c) 378 goals d) 478 goals

5. What did you learn from the fact box in the text?

____

Wayne Gretzky – Think About It! (cont.)

6 How did Wayne Gretzky feel about playing hockey?

a) He didn't like it at all.
b) He only played for fun sometimes.
c) He loved it so much it never felt like practicing.
d) He only played because his friends did.

7 What was one of Wayne Gretzky's character traits?

a) He was always grumpy.
b) He was a bad sport.
c) He had an incredibly accurate shot.
d) He never practiced.

8 How many NHL records did Wayne set or tie during his career?

a) 10 b) 25 c) 61 d) 100

9 Why do you think Wayne Gretzky set or tied so many NHL records?

a) He was very lucky.
b) He worked hard and was a talented player.
c) He cheated.
d) He had a lot of help from his teammates.

Wayne Gretzky – Think About It! (cont.)

An **interview** is a conversation between two people.
One person (the interviewer) asks questions.
The other person (the interviewee) answers them.

10 Pretend you are going to interview Wayne Gretzky. What are three questions you would ask him?

Draw a picture.

☐ I used capitals and end marks. ☐ My printing is neat. ☐ My writing makes sense.

Unit 22 Bugs: Pests or Friends?

When you see a bug, or insect, how do you feel? Do you like to watch it? Or do you think it is yucky? Some bugs hurt us, but we could not live without bugs.

Some Bugs Hurt Us

Some insects, such as mosquitos and fleas, bite and sting. Ouch! They may also spread diseases that hurt us. Other bugs, such as some beetles and grasshoppers, eat food that we grow. Termites and some ants even eat the wood in our houses!

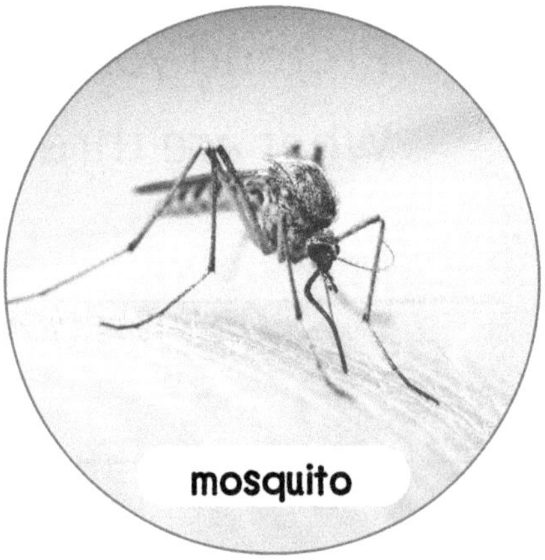

Some Bugs Help Us

Flies, beetles, and earthworms eat dead plants and dead animals. These bugs turn that waste into good soil. New plants can grow in the soil.

Some bugs, such as dragonflies, eat mosquitos. Ladybugs eat bugs that harm plants. How else do insects help us? Bees give us honey. They also give us wax to make floors shiny.

Bugs: Pests or Friends? – Think About It!

1. Colour the bugs that hurt us. blue
   Colour the bugs that help us. red
   Colour the bugs that eat food we grow. purple
   Colour the bugs that eat dead plants and animals. green

ladybug

mosquito

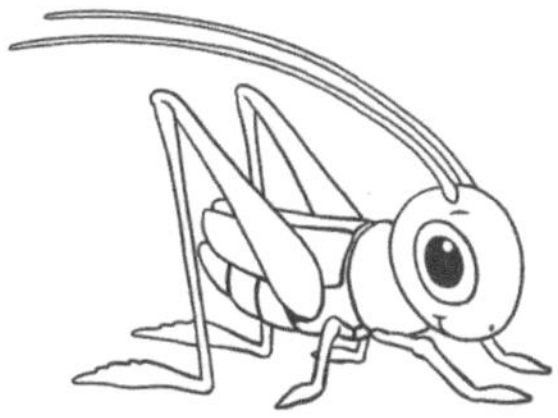

grasshopper

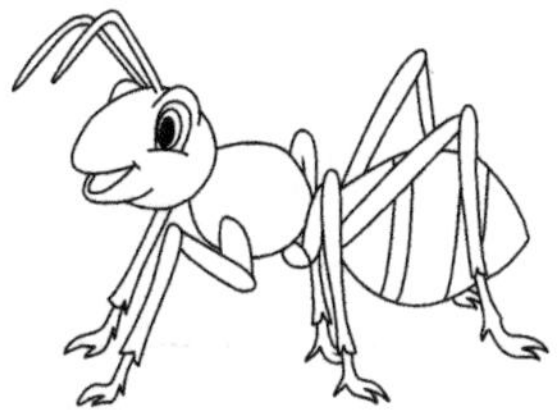

ant

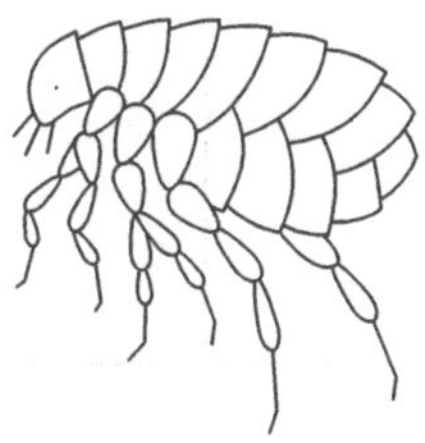

flea

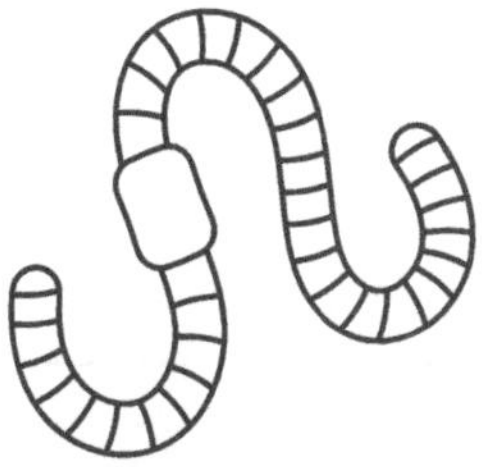

earthworm

beetle

honeybee

fly

2. When you see a bug, or insect, how do you feel?

____

____

Bugs: Pests or Friends? – Think About It! (cont.)

3 Fill out the chart below using information from the reading.

Ways Bugs Help Us	Ways Bugs Hurt Us

4 Sort the words according to the number of syllables.

beetle	bug	butterfly	flea	fly
insect	ladybug	honeybee	termite	

1 syllable	2 syllables	3 syllables
____________	____________	____________
____________	____________	____________
____________	____________	____________

Bugs: Pests or Friends? – Think About It! (cont.)

An **idiom** is a phrase that doesn't mean what it seems to mean. It has a special meaning that is different from the way it sounds.

5 Match each idiom on the left with its meaning on the right.

Ants in your pants ●	● A feeling of nervousness in your stomach
Busy as a bee ●	● A market where people sell used things
Butterfly in your stomach ●	● To get out of something by being sneaky
Worm your way out of something ●	● To be very busy and active
Flea market ●	● To be unable to sit still or stand quietly

Reading Challenge

Colour each box as you finish reading each text.

a book of poetry	a fairy tale	a book that teaches a lesson about life	a book with animals
a book that is part of a series	a magazine	a book that you read outside of class	realistic fiction
a book that teaches you how to do something	a book with a mystery	a book recommended by a friend	a book with an adventure
a non-fiction book	a fantasy	a story about a real person's life	a book you have read outloud to someone else
a chapter book	a picture book	an online article	a graphic novel or comic book

Reading Log - Books I Have Read

Book Title	Purpose of the Text	Rate This Book
	☐ to inform ☐ to entertain ☐ to persuade	☆ ☆ ☆ ☆
	☐ to inform ☐ to entertain ☐ to persuade	☆ ☆ ☆ ☆
	☐ to inform ☐ to entertain ☐ to persuade	☆ ☆ ☆ ☆
	☐ to inform ☐ to entertain ☐ to persuade	☆ ☆ ☆ ☆
	☐ to inform ☐ to entertain ☐ to persuade	☆ ☆ ☆ ☆
	☐ to inform ☐ to entertain ☐ to persuade	☆ ☆ ☆ ☆

Making Connections After Reading

Book Title: ______________________________

After reading...	It reminds me of...	This helps me make a connection to...
	something else I have read something about me the world around me	
	something else I have read something about me the world around me	

Book Review

Title: ______________________________

Author: ______________________________

MY RATING

☆ ☆ ☆ ☆

Author purpose: ☐ to inform ☐ to entertain ☐ to persuade

What was the book about?

____

Do you think other people would like the book? Explain your thinking.

____

____

____

____

Would you tell a friend to read the book? **YES** **NO**

☐ I used capitals and end marks. ☐ My printing is neat. ☐ My writing makes sense.

Reading Response

Title: ______________________________

This book is: ☐ Fiction ☐ Non-Fiction

Draw a picture of your favourite part of the book.

RATE THIS BOOK

☆ ☆ ☆ ☆

This is my favourite part of the book. Let me tell you why.

____

____

____

____

____

____

☐ I used capitals and end marks. ☐ My printing is neat. ☐ My writing makes sense.

That Reminds Me

Title: ____________________

This book reminds me of: 📖 something else I have read ◯ something about me 🌍 the world around me

Let me tell you why.

____

____

____

____

____

☐ I used capitals and end marks. ☐ My printing is neat. ☐ My writing makes sense.

Fact and Opinion

I read about this topic: ______________________________

✓ **Fact** A statement that can be proven to be true.
Opinion A feeling or belief about something.

☐ I used capitals and end marks. ☐ My printing is neat. ☐ My writing makes sense.

What Is Your Opinion?

Here is some advice:
You should treat people the way you want to be treated.

I (agree   disagree) with this advice. Let me tell you why.

First of all, ____

____

Another reason is, ____

____

Finally, ____

____

This is why I (agree   disagree) with this advice.

☐ I used capitals and end marks. ☐ My printing is neat. ☐ My writing makes sense.

Character Traits of ______________________

On the Outside (Physical Traits)

This is what we can see with our eyes.

Portrait

On the Inside (Personality Traits)

This is what we learn based on what the character says, does, and feels.

Story Recap

Title: ____

Who is the story about?

What happened in the story?

Where did the story take place?

How did the story end?

Recount Writing Planner

Who?	What?

When?	Where?	Why?

Title: ______________________

☐ I used capitals and end marks. ☐ My printing is neat. ☐ My writing makes sense.

BUY THIS ____________________ !

Cut and paste a picture from a magazine or flyer of something you would like to sell. Complete this advertisement to convince people to buy it.

Contact me at:

Selling Price:

Let me tell you why!

____

____

____

____

____

____

☐ I used capitals and end marks. ☐ My printing is neat. ☐ My writing makes sense.

WANTED!

For: ______________________

Please call:

Reward:

Who or what? ______________________

When last seen? ______________________

Where last seen? ______________________

Description: ______________________

____

____

☐ I used capitals and end marks. ☐ My printing is neat. ☐ My writing makes sense.

Write a Friendly Letter

DATE

Dear ____________,

GREETING

BODY

Sincerely,

CLOSING / SIGNATURE

☐ I used capitals and end marks. ☐ My printing is neat. ☐ My writing makes sense.

Poster Title: ____________________

Create a poster. What is the purpose of this poster?

☐ to give information ☐ to persuade ☐ to entertain

☐ I used capitals and end marks. ☐ My printing is neat. ☐ My message is clear.

Narrative Writing Planner

Narrative writing tells a story that has a beginning, a middle, and an end. It can be about something that actually happened, or it can be made up.

Title: ____

Setting: Where will the story take place?	**Characters:** Who will be in the story?
Problem in the Story: What is the problem in the story?	
Events in the Story: What happens in the story?	
How the Problem Is Solved: How does the story end?	

Write a Narrative

Title: ______________________________

Beginning

- ☐ I wrote an attention-grabbing first sentence.
- ☐ I introduced the main character(s) and included details.
- ☐ I wrote about where and when the story takes place.

____

____

____

____

____

____

____

____

☐	**Capitalization**	• Do my sentences and proper nouns have capital letters?
☐	**Organization**	• Did I order my ideas in a way that makes sense?
☐	**Punctuation**	• Do my sentences have end marks? (. ! ?)
☐	**Spelling**	• Did I check my spelling to the best of my ability?

Write a Narrative

Problem ☐ I explained the problem in the story.

____

____

____

____

Events

- ☐ I wrote about events that happen before the problem is solved.
- ☐ I told my story in order using the words **first**, **then**, and **next**.
- ☐ I added details to each event to show what was happening.

Event 1:

____

____

____

____

☐	**Capitalization**	• Do my sentences and proper nouns have capital letters?
☐	**Organization**	• Did I order my ideas in a way that makes sense?
☐	**Punctuation**	• Do my sentences have end marks? (**. ! ?**)
☐	**Spelling**	• Did I check my spelling to the best of my ability?

Write a Narrative

Event 2:

____

____

____

____

Ending ☐ I explained how the problem was solved.

Ending:

____

____

____

____

- ☐ **Capitalization** • Do my sentences and proper nouns have capital letters?
- ☐ **Organization** • Did I order my ideas in a way that makes sense?
- ☐ **Punctuation** • Do my sentences have end marks? (. ! ?)
- ☐ **Spelling** • Did I check my spelling to the best of my ability?

Congratulations!

Great Work!

Answers

Words with *l* Blends pp. 4–5

1. a) cl b) pl c) cl d) bl e) fl f) gl g) pl h) gl i) bl j) fl k) bl l) pl

2. a) clock b) plant c) slide d) glass e) sleep f) club g) plate h) clown i) fly j) gloves

Words with *r* Blends pp. 6–7

1. a) fr b) dr c) cr d) tr e) fr f) br g) pr h) br i) cr j) gr k) dr l) tr

2. a) crack b) broom c) green d) price e) drain f) fridge g) trunk h) drink i) trick j) crust

Words with *s* Blends pp. 8–9

1. a) sm b) sp c) sn d) sp e) sl f) sc g) sn h) sl i) sw j) sk k) sm l) st

2. a) spin b) stars c) skip d) scores e) skunk f) smoke g) sloth h) snack i) sticker j) swim

Words with *sh* pp. 10–11

1. a) shovel b) ship c) shoe d) leash e) washer f) cash g) fish h) shark i) bush j) shed

2. a) leash b) shovel c) fish d) shoes e) cash f) sharks g) washer h) shed i) ship j) bush

Words with *ck* pp. 12–13

1. a) lock b) clock c) kick d) sock e) duck f) bucket g) stick h) jacket i) rocket j) truck

2. a) duck b) kick c) clock d) sock e) bucket f) truck g) lock h) stick i) rocket j) jacket

Words with *th* and *wh* pp. 14–15

1. *th* words: both, father, moth, third, thumb
wh words: nowhere, pinwheel, wheat, when, why

2. Answers will vary.

3. a) wh b) th c) wh d) wh e) th f) th

4. a) tooth b) Who c) three d) Where

Words with *ch* and *tch* pp. 16–17

1. *ch* words: chin, chop, couch, much, which
tch words: fetch, hatch, itch, patch, pitch

2. Answers will vary.

3. a) tch b) ch c) ch d) tch e) ch f) tch

4. a) catch b) lunch c) ketchup d) March

Short Vowels pp. 19–21

1. a) a b) o c) e d) i e) u f) a g) e h) o i) i j) u k) a l) e

2. a) e b) i c) o d) u e) a f) e

3. a) pen b) bug c) net d) hat e) cup

4. short *a*: and, sat, zap short *e*: best, red, yes
short *i*: bill, sip, win short *o*: hot, job, stop short *u*: fun, hug, up

5. a) zap b) best c) hug d) bill e) red f) job

Long Vowels pp. 22–24

1. a) a b) e c) u d) i e) o f) e g) i h) a i) o j) u k) e l) i

2. a) u b) e c) o d) i e) e f) a

3. a) cube b) Pete c) kite d) cake e) bite f) use

4. long *a*: baby, late, wave long *e*: feel, here, neat
long *i*: hide, pipe, time long *o*: cone, hole, home
long *u*: huge, mule, unit

5. a) wave b) late c) hide d) hole e) feel f) neat

Short and Long Vowels p. 25

Red words: seal, note, beak, cube, dime, phone, paint, fire, rake, dice

Blue words: lap, mist, spell, fox, pot, sit, mug, bus, rat

Words with *ai*, *ay*, and *eigh* pp. 26–27

1. *ai* words: brain, drain, main, sail *ay* words: bay, say, today
eigh words: neighbour, sleigh, weight

2. Answers will vary.

3. a) play b) paint c) holiday d) nail e) clay f) tail

4. a) ai b) eigh c) ay

Words with *au* and *aw* pp. 28–29

1. *au* words: audio, author, haunt, launch, taught
aw words: dawn, draw, lawn, raw, yawn

2. Answers will vary.

3. a) au b) aw c) au d) aw e) aw f) au

4. a) sauce b) crawl c) yawn d) August

Words with *ee*, *ea*, and *ey* pp. 30–31

1. *ee* words: cheese, freeze, peel, tree
ea words: dream, each, tea *ey* words: honey, monkey, turkey

2. Answers will vary.

3. a) seed b) week c) steal d) road e) teeth f) meal

4. a) ee b) ea c) ey

Words with *ie* and *igh* pp. 32–33

1. *ie* words: die, flies, fries, tie *igh* words: bright, high, night, sight

2. Answers will vary.

3. a) tie b) fried c) right d) flies e) knight f) light

4. a) ie b) ie c) igh

Words with *y* as Long *i* and Long *e* Sounds pp. 34–35

1. *y* as long *i* words: buy, my, sky, try, why
y as long *e* words: bunny, jelly, lily, rainy, very

2. a) rainy b) fly c) money

3. a) long e b) long i c) long e d) long i e) long i f) long i g) long e h) long i i) long e j) long i k) long e l) long i

Answers

Words with *oa*, *oe*, and *ow* pp. 36–37

1. *oa* words: goal, oak, toad

ow words: below, crow, follow, grow *oe* words: doe, foe, toe

2. Answers will vary.

3. a) toast b) yellow c) glow d) blows e) throat f) hoe

4. a) oa b) ow c) oe

Words with *ui*, *ue*, and *ew* pp. 38–39

1. *ui* words: fruit, juice, suit *ue* words: blue, due, glue

ew words: knew, stew, threw

2. a) blue, glue b) stew, threw

3. a) due b) blew c) statue d) drew e) bruise f) suit

4. a) ui b) ew c) ue

Words with Silent *e* pp. 40–41

1. a) bat b) tub c) can d) plane e) tape f) kite g) hat h) note i) hug j) cube k) car l) mad

2. a) cute b) hat c) tube d) hope e) at f) can g) made

Words with *ar* and *or* pp. 42–43

1. a) fork b) barn c) star d) corn e) storm f) shorts g) park h) shark i) car j) forest

2. a) ar b) or c) ar d) or e) or f) ar

3. a) far b) card c) horse d) horn

Words with *er*, *ir*, and *ur* pp. 44–45

1. *er* words: otter, river, serve, water

ir words: circus, dirt, first, stir

ur words: burn, curl, hurt, nurse

2. Answers will vary

3. a) ur b) er c) ir d) er e) ur f) ir g) ur h) er i) ir j) er k) ir l) ur

Words with *oi* and *oy* pp. 46-47

1. *oi* words: choice, noise, point, spoil, voice

oy words: annoy, enjoy, royal, soy, toy

2. Answers will vary.

3. a) oi b) oy c) oi d) oy e) oy f) oi

4. a) oil b) loyal c) noisy d) destroy

Words with *ou* and *ow* pp. 48–49

1. *ou* words: about, count, hour, shout, sour

ow words: down, frown, how, howl, town

2. Answers will vary.

3. a) ow b) ou c) ow d) ou e) ou f) ow g) ow h) ow i) ou j) ow k) ou l) ou

Words with Long *oo* and Short *oo* Sounds pp. 50–51

1. short *oo* words: cook, foot, hook, wood

long *oo* words: food, moon, pool, tooth

2. Answers will vary.

3. a) spoon b) took c) Choose d) Look e) stool f) good

4. Red words: wood, book Yellow word: pool

Phonics Review pp. 53–55

1. a) ou b) igh c) ea d) ui e) or f) ey g) ir h) ur i) ue j) ir k) aw l) oi

2. a) ey b) ar c) eigh d) er e) ir f) oe g) au h) ou i) ui j) ea k) ar l) au

3. a) ow b) aw c) ew d) ie e) ee f) ar g) ay h) oa i) ea j) ie k) ui l) eigh

What Is a Sentence? p. 58

1. a) × b) ✓ c) ✓ d) × e) ✓ f) ×

2. Answers will vary.

Exploring Kinds of Sentences pp. 59–61

1. to 4. Answers will vary.

5. a) ? b) . c) ! d) ? e) ! f) . g) ?

What Is a Noun? p. 62

1. to 3. Answers will vary.

4. b) girl, mother, dog c) picture, crayons, markers d) flowers, garden e) shoes, laces f) hotdogs, hamburgers, lunches

Nouns: Am I a Person, Place, or Thing? p. 63

Red words: boy, teacher, mayor, student, nurse

Blue words: library, arcade, store, farm, park

Green words: book, fork, pencil, dog, toy, bread

Plural Nouns pp. 64–65

1. a) pigs b) trains c) jars d) snacks e) crayons f) drums

2. foot → feet goose → geese woman → women

3. a) foxes b) rulers c) cats d) beaches e) classes f) backpacks g) mugs h) boxes i) buses j) dresses

Pronouns: me, you, her, him, us, them, it pp. 66-67

1. a) She walked to the mall with him.

b) She waited for us.

2. a) She, Sarah b) He, Buster c) They, Jack and Jill d) It, ice cream e) We, Tim and I

Proper Nouns p. 69

1. Answers will vary.

2. Red words: Stacey, Fido, Tristan

Blue words: Canada, Oakville Mall, Toronto

Green words: Thursday, March, Monday

Yellow words: Christmas, New Year's Day, Valentine's Day

Nouns: Compound Words p. 70

1. backpack **2.** butterfly **3.** weekend **4.** airplane

Answers

Nouns: Compound Word Challenge p. 71

Possible answers: backpack, pancake, doghouse, beachball, mailbox, sandbox, sandman, cupcake, goldfish, rainbow, fireman, firehouse, firefly, jellyfish, sandcastle, mailman, toothbrush, snowball, snowman, housefly

Verbs: Simple Present Tense p. 73

1. a) sits b) jump c) shines d) hugs

2. Answers will vary. Sample: The children run after the ball.

Present Tense Verb: "To Be" p. 74

1. a) am b) are c) is d) is e) are f) are

2. a) Answers will vary. Sample: He is happy.
b) Answers will vary. Sample: The dog is fast.

Past Tense Verb: "To Be" p. 75

1. a) was b) were c) were d) was e) was f) were

2. a) Answers will vary. Sample: He was reading.
b) Answers will vary. Sample: Raindrops were falling.

Verbs: Using the Past Tense p. 76

1. called **2.** danced **3.** played **4.** raked **5.** helped **6.** washed

Verbs: Irregular Past Tense p. 77

1. a) fell b) rode c) ran d) left

2. a) slept b) flew c) found d) bought

Adjectives p. 78

1. Answers will vary.

2. a) blue b) fluffy c) happy d) big

3. Answers will vary.

Adjectives: Describing Nouns p. 79

Green words: pretty, dull, silly, cool, yellow, funny, pink, cold, blue, sharp, fast, warm

Adjectives: Describing Words p. 82

1. yummy, yellow, sweet

2. beautiful, large

3. smart, cheerful

4. funny, cool, friendly

5. smart, caring, nice

Articles: *A* and *An* p. 83

1. an **2.** a **3.** an **4.** a **5.** an **6.** a **7.** a **8.** a **9.** an

Red words: mitten, fish, net, sock, bat

Blue words: igloo, egg, owl, ant

Prepositions: Place p. 84

1. a) under b) with c) under d) under e) with

2. Answers will vary.

Prepositions: Time p. 85

1. a) before b) before c) after d) before e) after

2. Answers will vary.

Conjunctions: *And* p. 86

1. I brought a sandwich for lunch, and I ate it.

2. I like apples, and I like bananas.

3. I bought a toy car, and I bought a hockey stick.

4. I went to the waterpark, and I went to the museum.

Conjunctions: *But* p. 87

1. I wanted a spoon for cere t I only had a fork.

2. I painted a picture, but I lost it.

3. I wanted to play outside, but it was raining.

4. I wanted to play a game, but the computer did not work.

Contractions pp. 88–89

1.

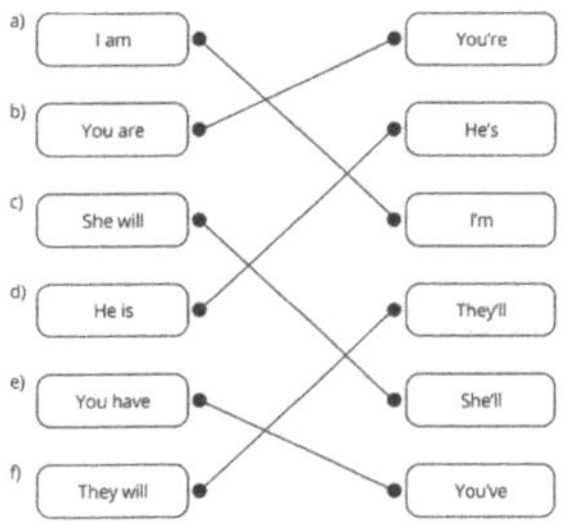

2.

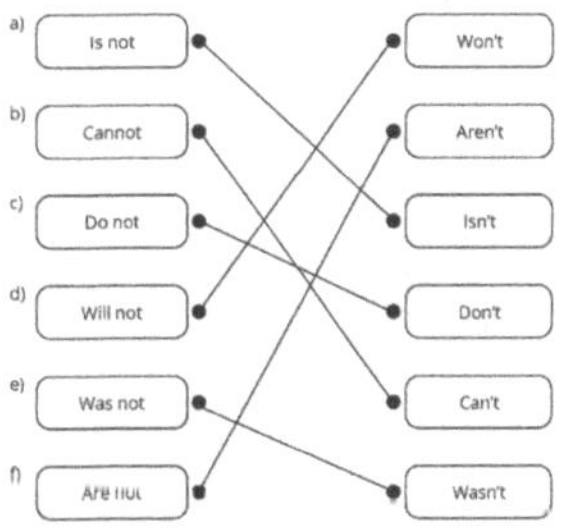

A Trip to the Zoo pp. 94–97

1. a **2.** b **3.** c **4.** d **5.** a

6. Katie's Mom → "Today we will go to the zoo."
Katie → "We are going to have a fun day!"

7. a) zoo b) umbrellas c) snakes d) fun

8. Answers will vary.

A Day at the Beach! pp. 98–101

1. b **2.** a **3.** b **4.** b **5.** b

7. 3, 6, 2, 4, 1, 5

8. Marco → "You must be Spot,"
Dog owner → "Has anybody seen a small white and brown dog?"

9. Answers will vary.

Answers

Plants Are All Around pp. 102–105

1. c **2.** a) nests b) tulip c) many d) food e) sea turtles

3. a **4.** d **5.** c **6.** Answers will vary.

7. Answers will vary.

The Lost Keys pp. 106–109

1. Her lost keys. **2.** b **3.** a **4.** c **5.** b

6. Answers will vary.

7. Yolanda → lost her keys before going to school

Yolanda's mom → helped look for the lost keys

8. Answers will vary. **9.** Answers will vary.

Occupations: X-ray Technician pp. 110–113

1. a **2.** c **3.** b **4.** c **5.** b **6.** d

7.

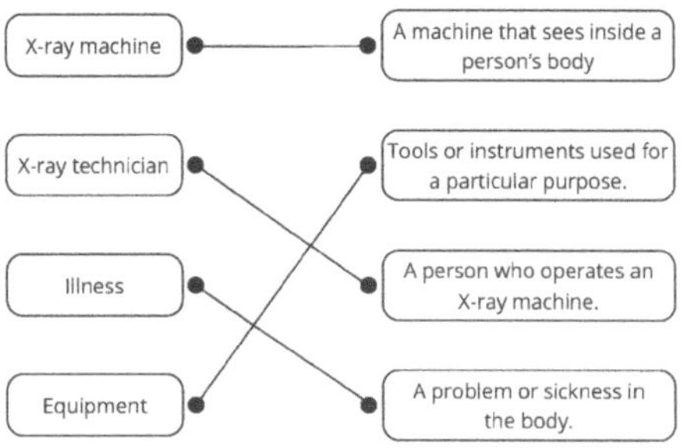

8. Answers will vary.

Occupations: Air Traffic Controller pp. 114–117

1.

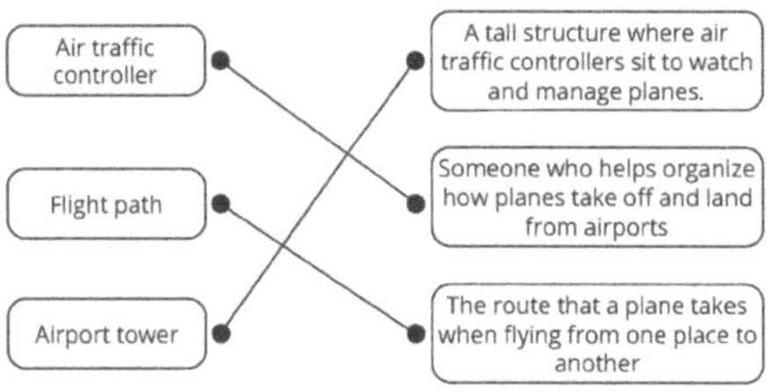

2. c **3.** b **4.** a **5.** b **6.** b **7.** b **8.** a **9.** a)

10. Answers will vary.

Aisha Goes to a New School pp. 118–121

1.

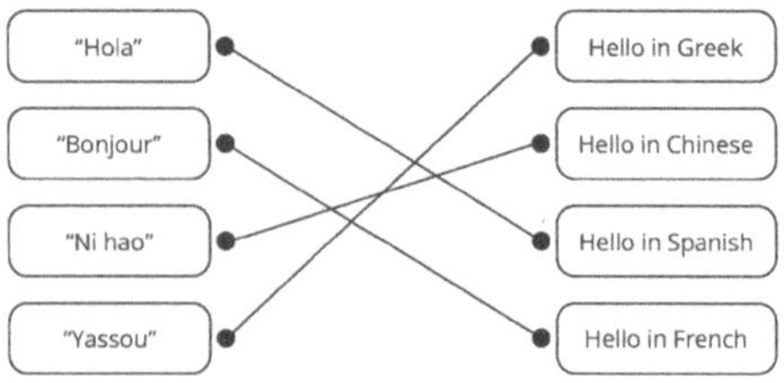

2. a) anyone b) Syria c) chips d) Spanish

3. Answers will vary. **4.** Answers will vary.

Meet Max: My Furry and Friendly Dog pp. 122–125

1. a) furry b) golden c) fluffy d) wet e) kind f) shiny g) floppy h) wag i) handsome j) cute

2. Answers will vary. **3.** Answers will vary.

How Do You Like Them Apples? pp. 126–129

1. a) opinion b) fact c) fact d) fact e) fact

2.

A	P	P	L	E	L	Y	P
R	O	U	N	D	K	L	J
T	R	E	E	A	O	I	U
U	H	N	A	T	U	R	E
V	I	T	A	M	I	N	S
S	W	E	E	T	Q	W	E
H	G	E	D	S	O	U	P

3. b **4.** c **5.** c

6. Answers will vary. Sample: They grow on trees.

7. Answers will vary. Sample: They taste different.

8. to 10. Answers will vary.

Thumper Makes a Friend pp. 130–133

1. 2, 1, 3 **2.** b **3.** b **4.** c **5.** Answers will vary.

6. Title: Thumper Makes a Friend

Setting: The forest

Characters: Thumper and the bird

Problem: The little bird had fallen out of its nest.

Solution: Thumper hopped up to the nest and put the bird back.

7. Answers will vary.

Save Water to Help Your Planet! pp. 134–137

1. a) solution b) problem

2. a) tap b) shower c) bucket d) healthy

3. Answers will vary. **4.** Answers will vary.

Fun After School: A Day in the Life of Jack pp. 138–141

1. a **2.** b **3.** c **4.** b **5.** Answers will vary.

6. First: Jack went to the park with his mom.

Next: They walked back home.

Then: They baked some oatmeal cookies.

Finally: Jack played outside with his friends.

7. Answers will vary.

Billy's Flat Tire pp. 142–145

1. 3, 4, 2, 1

Answers

2.

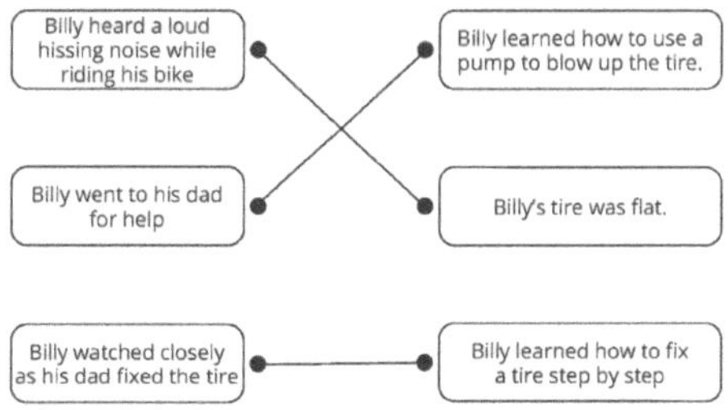

3. a) ride b) hissing c) flat d) pump e) fix

4. Answers will vary. **5.** Answers will vary.

How to Make a Cake pp. 146–149

1. yummy, taste buds dance

2. a) water, oil, eggs b) greased c) frosting, sprinkles d) yummy
e) happy

3. First, mix the cake batter. Next, bake the cake.
Then, decorate the cake. Finally, enjoy the cake.

4. Answers will vary.

Delicious Bannock pp. 150–153

1. b

2. Some baked their bannock in clay or rock ovens. Others wrapped the dough around a stick and toasted it. Some First Nations groups rolled their bannock in sand then baked it in a fire pit.

3. They taught Canada's explorers and fur traders how to make it.

4. Flour, baking powder, oil, and water. Sometimes people add spices or dried fruit and flavouring.

5. Powwows, rodeos, and festivals.

6. Cornmeal and ground plant bulbs → Long ago
Flour, baking powder, oil and water → Today

7. 1 syllable: clay, oil, stick
2 syllables: bannock, nation, spices
3 syllables: explorer, festival, rodeo

8. Answers will vary.

Dinosaur Park pp. 154–157

1. b **2.** d

3.

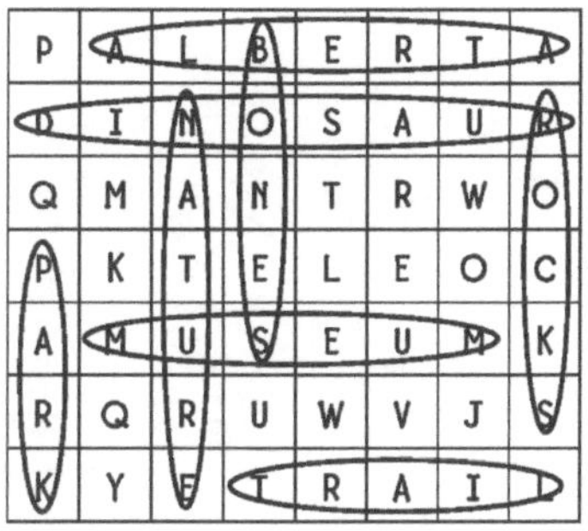

4. b **5.** a **6.** b **7.** a **8.** b **9.** b

10. Answers will vary.

Similies pp. 158–161

1. b

2. a) as soft as a blanket b) like fireworks
c) as white as a polar bear's fur d) as smart as a fox
e) like arms reaching up to the sky

3. Answers will vary. **4.** Answers will vary.

5.

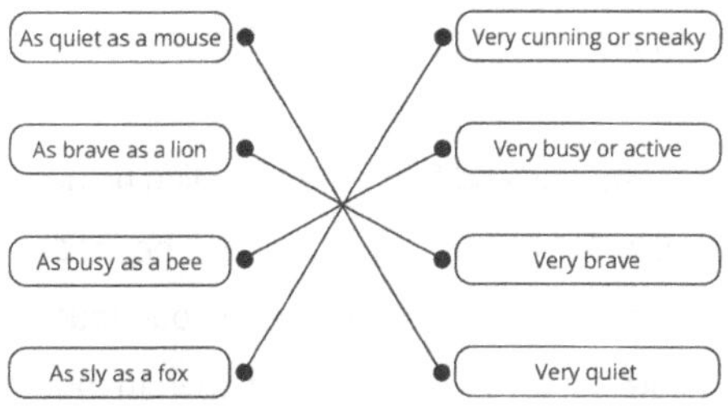

6. Answers will vary.

Earth Day pp. 162–165

1. b **2.** a **3.** b **4.** c **5.** a

6. to 8. Answers will vary.

Dinosaurs Big and Small pp. 166–169

1. T-Rex and Dilong

2. b **3.** a

4. Effect: Scientists can tell how big a dinosaur was.
Cause: Scientists look at a dinosaur's bones.

5. T-Rex and Dilong: many strong teeth, hunted animals for food
Only Dilong: had feathers when older, arms helped it eat

6. a) True b) False c) True d) False e) False f) True g) False

7. Answers will vary.

Occupations: Baker pp. 170–173

1. d **2.** c

3. a) recipe b) cupcakes, doughnuts c) bakery

4.

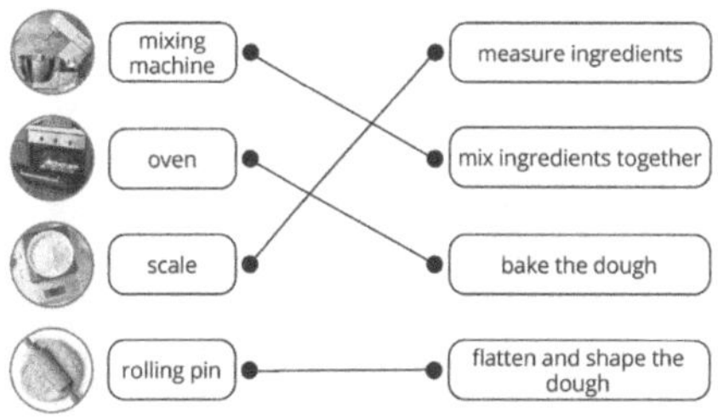

5. Fact, opinion **6.** Answers will vary. **7.** Answers will vary.

Wayne Gretzky pp. 174–177

1. a **2.** d **3.** b **4.** c

Answers

5. That Wayne Gretzky's jersey #99 was retired by all the teams in the NHL.

6. c **7.** c **8.** c **9.** b **10.** Answers will vary.

Bugs: Pests or Friends? pp. 178–181

1. Blue colour: mosquito, flea
Red colour: ladybug, earthworm, beetle, fly, ant
Purple colour: grasshopper, beetle
Green colour: ant, earthworm, beetle, fly

2. Ways Bugs Help Us: Flies, beetles, and earthworms eat dead plants and animals and turn them into good soil for plants to grow in.
Ways Bugs Hurt Us: Mosquitos and fleas bite and sting us and can spread diseases. Beetles and grasshoppers eat the foods we grow, and termites and ants can eat the wood in our houses.

3. Answers will vary, ensure students write information from the reading.

4. 1 syllable: bug, flea, fly
2 syllables: beetle, insect, termite
3 syllables: butterfly, honeybee, ladybug

5.

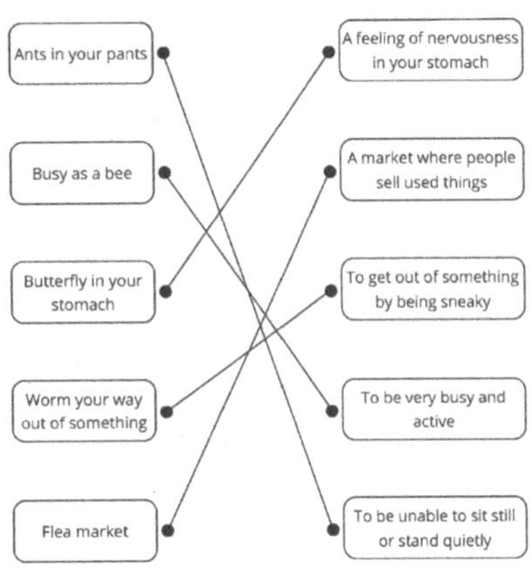